Good Eggs & Odd Fish

Also by Richard Stanton and published by Ginninderra Press
Enngonia Road
Seven Car Loads of What You Need
Under Firethorn

Other books by Richard Stanton
When Your Partner Dies (Allen & Unwin)
Media Relations (Oxford University Press)
All News Is Local (McFarland)
Do What They Like (Australian Scholarly Publishing)
Corporate Strategic Communication (Palgrave)

Richard Stanton

Good Eggs & Odd Fish

For Doc, Small, Johnboy, Medi, Bones and Bird

'When finds of wondrous treasure
Set all the South ablaze
And you and I were faithful mates
All through the roaring days!'
– Henry Archibald Lawson

Good Eggs & Odd Fish
ISBN 978 1 76109 587 0
Copyright © text Richard Stanton 2023
Cover image and chapter decorations: Peter Browne

First published 2023 by
Ginninderra Press
PO Box 3461 Port Adelaide 5015
www.ginninderrapress.com.au

Contents

Introduction	7
Image	11
Memory	15
Dreams & Fantasies	25
Music & Sex	30
Relationships	33
Dating Sites & Apps	37
Mates	41
Fathers & Sons	45
Well-being	50
Food	56
Sport	60
Television	65
Your Car	70
Entertainment	76
The Four-hour Rule	80
Volunteering	84
Men's Organisations	87
Religion	90
Politics	95
Commodities	103
Income & Investments	106
Pride & Prejudice	112
Negotiate & Navigate	117
Change Up & Change Down	122
It Is What It Is	126

Ratbags	129
Coronavirus	132
Forgiveness	137
Death	143
Conclusions & Intentions	149

Introduction

My great-grandfather, born a hundred years before me, married twice. After bearing three children, his first wife died at a relatively early age. Luckily for me, he remarried and his second wife had another seven, one of whom was my grandfather. If my great-grandfather had lolled about being depressed and not picked himself up, dusted himself off and found a new bride, I would not have got a run. He died aged seventy-one. Here's another one. He has been dead for a hundred years. Nowadays, hundreds figure widely in age calculations. If you don't live to, or expect to live to, at least ninety-five, you're not really trying. Well, I've made it to seventy and I can see the horizon. It's pretty damn close. I can't imagine living another twenty-five years. I will revisit my ancestors a bit later. Let's have a closer look at the present.

I don't know how to be seventy. Not that I knew how to be sixty or even fifty. But seventy? I thought I was going to know exactly how to work it. For a few months before the auspicious day, I planned and thought about how it would all play out. It would be a time to part with a whole lot of stuff, time to become someone who had done things and seen things and experienced things, so that whatever came after was going to be pretty good but not necessarily aligned with things that had already been. It was going to be a new dawn. A brave new world.

Well, let me tell you, it didn't work out that way. Not that things have gone wrong. I don't mean that. There's really nothing to complain about. Well, nothing major. I don't have any long-term illnesses, I don't take regular medication for anything sinister. I navigated my three score years and ten pretty well, considering. A bit of sickness as a kid – a year of rheumatic fever from one to two that culminated in a heart murmur which must have been mortifying for my poor mother; stupid hepatitis around ten which meant missing six weeks of school and never really catching up; constant bronchitis in winters from the damp and cold and fog of living near a river; busted teeth; then a bout of ulcerative colitis which hospitalised me before I had dispensed one score of those years. Again, nothing major, no poliomyelitis or meningitis, although we were given to believe that we could get those things pretty easily if we didn't watch out. Well, we watched out, got vaccinated and didn't see anyone contract them.

A pretty severe case of acne during the last years of high school was probably worse than anything, probably not worse than getting killed after getting knocked off your bike like one kid did when he rode down the main street and a car door opened in front of him, flinging him into the path of an oncoming car. And not as bad as flogging your old FJ down a steep hill a few days after your seventeenth birthday and crashing it into a tree and killing yourself, like another kid did. But it was pretty bad. When the big ones on your back and neck popped and left blood and pus on your shirt in class. When all you wanted to do was hide from the world, and the stress of having it made it worse. Things like that made it impossible to concentrate in class, which meant at the all-important pointy end you only managed to pass a couple of subjects.

When I look back on it now, it was the end of the 1960s but mercifully it was also the end of the first score. Not that things were all bad in those first twenty years. There was plenty of cricket. There was a first car, a powder-blue Morris Mini 850 that cost how much I have no idea. Can't remember. We'll come back to memory, but for now let's say that the cost of the car was much more than the weekly pay packet, which was $18. But I saved up and bought it and my dad drove me to where it was for sale and the bloke I bought it from was really nice and really old – probably around thirty – and his wife had just had a baby so he had to get rid of it and get something with four doors. Get rid of the Mini, not the baby. The baby didn't have four doors.

There was cricket every weekend in summer and in those days summer was long and pretty hot. Penrith wasn't called a western suburb of Sydney in those days. It was Penrith and there was a space between towns. If you drove from Penrith to Sydney, you went along the Great Western Highway through other small towns – Kingswood, St Marys, Mt Druitt, Rooty Hill, Wentworthville, Parramatta – and only after passing Parramatta did you drive into the urban continuity along Parramatta Road, until you arrived at Broadway, where you drove down passed the breweries and the lights into George Street. You could park there then. I had a mate a few years older than me who had a 1966 Cortina and we could get from Penrith to Moore Park on Saturday morning in fifty-five minutes for a nine o'clock cricket game. Don't ask me how, but we did.

I'm getting off the track a bit. Let's come back later and reminisce. We need to think more about what it is we have, now that we've reached seventy, and what we are going to do with it. As I wrote, I don't know how to be seventy. I thought I was going to know. Coronavirus got in the way and crashed any celebration that might have marked the occasion. A few mates delivered belated bottles of whisky, and another's wife knitted me a beaut woollen beanie, but more generally everyone went on with their business and now it's pretty much forgotten. The milestone of turning seventy, that is. Forgotten by everyone except me. I'm struggling with the fact that time has passed and I still don't know what to do. Soon I will be the same age as my great-grandfather when he died. There are only two of my direct male descendants who made it beyond that age – my father was eighty-one and my great-great-grandfather was also eighty-one. Every other male in a direct line from three hundred years ago has not got past seventy-two.

Here's what's happening now. It would be very easy to get angry about being powerless; the attacks being made on men, especially old white men, for perpetrating all the wrongs and evils that have occurred in the world since the beginning of time. It would be easy to sit in the club drinking schooners and whinging about how the 'feminazis' and 'lefties' control the media and education and there's nothing you can do about it any more. We get bashed up everywhere else, so that table near the pokies looks pretty good any time after three o'clock in the afternoon. There's always one or two like-minded souls crying into their bruisers.

Let's examine all the things that are going on for us as seventy-year-olds and put them in perspective, so that we may not only survive to make it to four score years, but flourish and continue to be what we ought to be – men.

Image

How do you see yourself and how do others see you? It's a shock to the system when you look at yourself in the mirror and see your father staring back at you, or some other old man that is not you. Or is not the you you think you are. Or feel. How you feel is how you act. Or not. A lot of seventy-year-olds remain active and fit. They cycle and run and play plenty of sport. Or at least games. Golf and bowls and tennis are games, not sport. Cricket is also a game. You look out at the world through the lens of the physical person you are. If that means being active, then you are active. If it means being passive, then you are passive. If it means being disabled or incapacitated, then that's who you are. At the time. It may not be all the time. Things may change. You may go from being very active to being disabled in the blink of an eye. And you may well recover and become active again. It doesn't really matter much. Everything slows down. As I write, a mate is fishing off Montague Island on the far south coast of NSW. Another is riding his e-bike along the bike track beside the Parramatta River in Sydney with a couple of other old, ugly, cranky blokes. Another still is at home waiting to have his corona booster – the vaccine, not the clear bottle of Mexican lolly water. Meanwhile, another was preparing to tee off after a good recovery from a quadruple heart bypass. How they see themselves is not necessarily how others see them.

As we age, we seek more comfort. We want comfortable shoes, a comfortable shirt, a comfortable chair. That about sums it up. And shorts. The poet Les Murray said he wished he lived somewhere where he could wear shorts all year. How good would that be? Shorts and thongs. Standard issue. Flappy shorts with plenty of room. Not that there's much to need room for in the package department. Shorts and thongs appear on younger blokes too. But they look different. Tight shorts and expensive Havvies. And while we wear the same pair of shorts around the house, on the golf course, to Bunnings and to the surf club, these younger blokes have different pairs for different situations. Work shorts – brown with black pockets; golf shorts, running shorts, really long shorts with FX emblazoned on the side for skaties and mountain biking, and tight shorts for road biking. Probably a lot of others as well. Compartmentalising activities requires a lot of different clothing. One pair of Aldi cargo shorts is not going to do it for them.

A good mate's older sister has been in a long-term relationship. She has three adult children, if that's what you call three people who no longer live with you or see you very much but expect you to be there when they need stuff. Anyway, for many years she has been living with a bloke who is not the father of her kids and recently, as he approached seventy, he began to change his behaviour. Nothing too obnoxious, so my mate said, just a few adjustments to make his life more comfortable. Like golf five times a week and fishing the other two because he lives near a golf course and a river and because he can. Well, things got a bit heated over Christmas lunch so the mate's sister says, 'If he's going to become Mr Grumpy, he's out of here.' Now this appears to be a bit extreme. Surely this fella is entitled to a quiet hit and an even quieter angle if the mood takes him and not to become the subject of a threat of eviction if, for example, he doesn't catch fish, or, worst-case scenario, he four-putts one green. Either of these events is likely to create a bit of grumpiness. I'm not sure it's deserving of the response. It's normal to expect a vicious aside or comeback from a member of the Millennial generation; after all, they see you as a waste of space, one they have to support with their taxes, if they pay taxes.

Another woman I know says she can stand in her kitchen all day and watch her husband out in the family room as he sits and stares at his computer screen without even knowing she is there. She says she could be naked and he wouldn't notice. As a seventy-year-old, she says, he has an image of himself that is pretty close to average. He's been married long enough so that if he ignores her she will simply get on with her own stuff and he can sit all day looking at his screen. She says he is conscious of nothing more than himself and what he wants to do and gets hurt if she castigates him for not paying her any attention. The question is whether this is indeed a standard relationship for a seventy-year-old man or is it an aberration? Is this an image of self that allows the individual to feel comfortable doing whatever he wants to do, assuming of course that there is no longer a work commitment, without being concerned for a partner or a relationship?

As we age, the importance of image should not be underestimated. The self as a seventy-year-old receives a lot of negativity from a variety of sources, even if we're not always aware that it is being directed at us. I was in a clothing shop recently thinking it might be nice to buy a new suit for a wedding that was imminent. I looked at a few racks, then a sales assistant, probably in her mid-forties, came over. She gave her little talk about sizes and which suits might look nice on me until I said I thought the 'slim' fit would look a little silly given I had for years been a forty-four regular. She gave me a jacket to try and it was too small. She said I was a forty-six, which is not the case. It's like shoe sizes. For years, I was no more than a nine but now a ten and a half only just fits. Funny how feet and chests grow in size as you age. Anyway, she went on about how good the suits looked on me no matter which one I tried until I said I didn't think a seventy-year-old could wear the slim fit.

'You're not seventy,' she said. 'You're not all hunched and bent over like a seventy-year-old. You're still straight and standing upright.' She proceeded to demonstrate what a seventy-year-old male should look like. I am interpreting most of what she said because English in her accent was difficult to discern.

The point of this is not that I didn't end up buying a new suit as I could see no use for it beyond the wedding, it is that we are stereotyped in everything we do from how we look to how we walk. And there is no joy in someone telling us we don't look like seventy-year-olds because we don't shuffle and stoop. What do we look like then? Sixty-year-olds? Fifty-year-olds? Doubtful. If the shop assistant didn't think I was seventy, what did she think? Probably nothing. She didn't actually think about me at all. I was a male customer looking at suits. Nothing more. She dug deeply into her bag of customer relations and all she could dredge up was an image of a stooped shuffler who probably smelled bad.

Memory

Memory is a tricky thing. In our first few years of life, we watch everything and learn how to do stuff by mimicking those we most often see. Throughout history, baby boys have become men by watching their fathers and mothers and learning how to perform simple and complicated actions. We learn how to walk and talk and read and write, and add up and subtract, and run and jump, and we apply these skills throughout life, sometimes in more complex ways, often times in the same simple way we learned them. We also become aware of danger and risk – how far we could jump, how far we could run, how far we could push boundaries before we were told to stop or to look out, or some other caution that framed what we did. We learned a lot and we retained it until it began to seem like we no longer remembered what we learned. And it took longer to do the same thing because we became physically less able. So while we were slowing down physically and taking longer to do stuff, or being more cautious about how we did stuff so we didn't bust a boiler, our minds also began to slow. We began to forget the names of people we went to school with, whereas not long ago we could look at a high school photo and name everyone in the class. Then it seemed as if, all of a sudden, we could no longer link a face with a name. We justified it by saying to ourselves that it was no longer important, we had other things on our minds. But it was a creeping memory loss that affected everything we did and how we were perceived. But this was not the end of it. If it had been a gradual loss of cognitive function by itself, we could have managed it. Who cares if you can't remember who you went to school with more than fifty years ago? No one. Unless you lived in a small town and stayed put, then you probably never again saw those people you went to school with so long ago. By now, many of them are probably dead. Not everyone lives beyond seventy. More importantly, you could deal with the cognitive loss if you were not forced by generational change to re-learn everything as if you were again a two-year-old.

What I mean by this is simple. And it can be distilled into one word. Change. Throughout our lives, we learned skills and rituals, we learned things that were practical necessities and we learned societal skills. In other words, we learned how to be men and how to engage. Society did not impose upon us how we ought to do certain things. They were learned experiences. Some of us failed to learn. Some us failed to grasp societal mores; the rules that govern Western society. Which is why we have a prison system. Not every man in prison suffers from a mental illness which made him do evil.

Now here we are, having navigated three score years and ten, feeling that our achievements, however large or small, might give us some leeway when it comes to the last few years of our lives. But no. Instead, we are confronted by the spectre of being told we are responsible for all the wrongs that have been perpetrated on the world since the beginning of Western civilisation. Combine this with the notion that everything we established, or were part of establishing, is being wiped away by a new generation in power, then no wonder we feel isolated, angry and alone.

We are pretty adaptable. But when it comes to changing the game and we have to readapt by learning everything over again, then it's understandable that we get a bit cranky. But we're not allowed to do that. Get cranky, I mean. The rules have changed so much that what we thought we knew and what might once have been sentimentally referred to as old ways, no longer exist. We can blame technology but it's far more sinister than a computer manufacturer making you buy a new computer because your old one no longer has enough space or won't work with one of the new 'social media' platforms or Microsoft 'teams'. The changes being wrought are what they call systemic. This is a cute way of saying everything is being defenestrated and we are starting again from scratch without any acknowledgement of what worked in the past. Basically, it means eliminating everything to do with the us. Us seventy-year-olds, that is.

I mentioned earlier not being able to remember how much I paid for my first car. Fifty years have gone by since I fell in love with it and wanted it so much. So it's not surprising that I don't recall. What is surprising is the way the mind works. I can't remember the cost of it but I remember as clear as crystal the day I blew it up on the road between Young and Cowra. I had been visiting someone in Tumut for the weekend. I left mid-Sunday afternoon to drive the six or seven hours home when coming into Young the engine started making a clattering sound. I pulled in to what looked like a mechanic's workshop and there was a bloke there on duty pumping petrol. He listened to the noise and we agreed it was probably tappets. So off I went, but not for long. About forty kilometres later, there was an almighty bang, the gearstick shot up and hit the roof, bits of engine clunked onto the road and things pretty much came to a standstill. Sunday arvo is ominously quiet in that part of the world, or it was in the early 1970s. I got out and looked back. There was a long oil slick and bits of metal strewn for a hundred metres. I opened the bonnet and, sure enough, there was a piston-sized hole in the side of the engine block. And a piston on the road. A hunk of metal about fifty millimetres by fifty millimetres with the engine number stamped on it lay quietly on the gravel shoulder. So it wasn't tappets.

Turned out the big-end bearing had seized. Poor little guy wasn't up to such a long drive. A car eventually came the other way and stopped to see if I was okay. I gave the driver a dollar note and asked if they would call the NRMA when they arrived at Young. A telephone call in those days cost a lot less than a dollar but I thought they might need an incentive. A dollar was a fair whack for someone who earned $18 a week. After a few further hours of anxiety and stress, I was preparing to either walk on to Cowra or back to Young or bed down for the night by the side of the road when a tow truck arrived from Young. Relief. A short time later, we arrived in Young and the truck driver promised to keep the Mini safe until I could get back to collect it. There was no point talking about repairs being done there – it needed a new engine.

A few hours later, with my bag, I waited on the railway station for a train to Sydney. I have no idea how much it cost, what time it arrived or any details other than it pulled in to Central Station sometime in the early dawn of Monday morning. I flopped on to the Blue Mountains train and made my way home. It was Monday and I was supposed to be going to work in the city. Lucky for me, I was at that stage of my life a public servant, so a Monday sickie was par for the course.

My dad, bless his heart, organised with a mate of his to borrow a car trailer which we then towed the following week over the mountains and on down to Cowra. Dad had a 1969 Valiant VE Regal sedan, white with red vinyl upholstery. It was a beauty, built by Chrysler in South Australia. But he had frequent trouble with the welsh plugs. Probably something to do with the hemi or 'slant' engine that sat sideways. I knew what welsh plugs were because I had watched and assisted where I could when he frequently changed them. They seemed to leak even after shortish drives so you can imagine the pressure placed on them towing a trailer over the mountains. Well, as luck would have it, they held until we got to Young, pushed and shoved the poor old Mini onto the trailer then began heading home. It was meant to be a day trip. We had set out early in anticipation of a longish drive then a longer one home slowly towing the dead blue beast. Outside Cowra, plans changed. The engine temperature went off the grid so we stopped to check. Sure enough. A welsh plug. The garage at Cowra was ready to close but he said he could fix it early next morning. My poor father.

Seems like his life was just a series of rescue and retrieval events that involved his son. Which was probably a fair balance, as he had very little to do with me when I was younger. We might cover that later.

For now, it's memory that we're interested in. The question is, which bits of memory stay and which vanish? I can remember staying in Cowra, but not about getting the Valiant fixed the next day nor the drive home from there. I also remember bunging a reconditioned short motor, which I could not really afford, in the Mini but it was never the same. I got rid of it a few years later and upgraded to a yellow Clubman. From 850cc to 1100. What a power surge. Now I drive a six-litre SS Holden. Who would have guessed, way back then?

So here I am remembering the blown motor, the Chrysler Valiant and various other bits and pieces but lost, or lingering in the fog of the past, are other assorted pieces of information related to the events.

For example, I went to Tumut to visit a girl I had met through a mate in Canberra. She invited me for the weekend. On the Sunday, we ate the biggest lunch I had ever seen. Her father and brothers hoed in to huge plates of tucker. They were farmers, I was a skinny, six-foot twenty-year-old who until then thought he could eat. What's puzzling, though, is why I went there in the first place and, after the event, why I never saw that girl again. Perhaps she wondered the same thing for a week or two.

And on the run to pick up the car, our old curmudgeonly neighbour came with us. I remember him standing at the fence when we were preparing to leave saying how much he missed his earlier life in Bombala and he wished he could come with us to see how the countryside looked these days. Well, stupid as he was, we were even stupider. We said, why not come? He huffed and puffed for a while then his wife, who hated him hanging around whingeing, said yes, go. So he couldn't back out. But all I recall of his presence was the constant whingeing and whining and then when we were stuck in Cowra for the night how much louder the whining got. I don't think we spoke to him all the next day and before long his wife chucked him out. I remember that because there was an almighty shouting match that went on for hours.

The question is, why do we remember or recall some events, or parts of events, and not others as we age? What part of those two events is important to my seventy-year-old mind while other events and occasions slide away, never to resurface? I don't have an answer. What I do remember are things that happened at various times over the past fifty years and less so in the earlier years before that, from childhood to early twenties. Some early things stick. And some mid-range things that pop in at bizarre times such as four o'clock in the morning after having to get up to wee. Back in bed, it's as if the memory stick in my head is whirring around jamming at random spots. It's as if memory wants these things to surface but has no idea why it wants them to. One example is interesting but not interesting enough to spend time trying to analyse it. But it was something that is now impossible to do.

I was on a flight from Sydney to Hong Kong in the early 1990s. In those days, you could ask a stewardess (now a flight attendant) for things and she would bring them and have a chat about stuff. It might have been a last beer before we prepared for landing. These days, you're lucky to find an attendant, let alone get a cold ale at any time during a flight. We got to chatting about something or other and I asked if it was possible to go up to the flight deck (some airlines still call it a cockpit even though they have women pilots). She went off to ask the skipper and before I knew it I was sitting in the third officer's seat with the pilot and co-pilot introducing themselves and explaining what goes on at the controls. Simple really. Press a button or two and the huge hurtling metal coffin sails on through the blue. I must have seemed enthusiastic, because they let me stay there for quite some time. And before long, we were at the last way-point that put us on a bearing into Hong Kong airport. This was the old airport in the middle of the city, not the one the Chinese government built offshore by flattening a perfectly good island. As we hit the descent bearing, I thought the pilot would shunt me out but no, he said it was too late to go back to my seat so I might as well buckle up and stay for the ride. Boy oh boy and what a ride it was.

There was a crosswind and the tunnel down which the Boeing 747 had to traverse seemed narrower than an Italian side street – barely big enough to drive a Fiat Panda through. As we got closer, the high-rise buildings got bigger and bigger until we were roaring along five degrees off centre on a downward trajectory focused on a tiny piece of tarmac that looked as if it was impossible to land on. Rather than being scared witless, I was ecstatic. The pilots did this every day so it was routine. There was no risk, or what little risk there was remained manageable. For me, however, it was spectacular. Here we were travelling at enormous speed, pointed at the ground but with the possibility of veering off into one of the apartment blocks at any second. It was not to be. The bomber burst out of the corridors of grey washing-laden balconies into clear airfield space and then with what appeared to be expert judgement (which it was) we were thudding wheels down into the middle of Hong Kong. The pilot and co-pilot exchanged looks. You okay, they asked? Never better. Like a toddler filled with glee, I wanted them to go back and do it again. More please? As we taxied to the dock, the very nice attendant came and got me. She made me feel very special as she escorted me back to my seat, got my luggage from the overhead locker, gave me a big smile and wished me safe travels. Bloody hell. What an experience.

While my memory disk locked on to that anecdote, it was also working its way around trying to find similar experiences (experiences now have the added value of being referred to as 'lived' experiences). It stopped at another image that involved speed and risk but in slightly different circumstances. I had been employed as a journalist on a business magazine in the early to mid-1980s and on occasion got to go off on junkets. Some were good, others pretty mundane. You can get a bit sick of travelling all the way from Australia to England, or America or Europe to look at stuff like earthmoving equipment or computers. In those days, computers and information technology was relatively new – no smartphones, no internet as we now know it. So going off to California for a computer expo for a week was pretty big stuff. Or being invited by the world's largest earthmoving equipment manufacturer to go to a construction expo in Las Vegas with a stopover on return in Hawaii for a few days because the trip had been so 'arduous'. On another occasion, I travelled to England to look at some construction sites and equipment. The trip was paid for by the British consulate. Business class airfares and accommodation in a top-class hotel in London, all provided with no strings, simply the possibility that I might find it interesting enough to write about. These trips were all very nice and all part of the 1980s business popularity model. Corporations were being taken over by flamboyant operators such as John Elliot, Chris Skase and Alan Bond; Bob Hawke had come to political power and the world was up for grabs. At least until 1987.

For a variety of reasons, one of those junkets sticks out more than others, or remains in my memory more clearly. I was invited by Volvo, the Swedish automotive manufacturer, to travel to Sweden and Europe to test drive its new car. This was in early 1986. Volvo had developed a new model, still like a box, but a different box to the older models. They were taking a group of Australian motoring writers to do the test drive and someone in the company thought it would be a good idea to also take a business journalist. The magazine I worked for was the pre-eminent business journal of the day – others would come along later but would never have quite the same cachet. The trip was for ten days flying Singapore Airlines business class from Sydney to Copenhagen, then SAS to Gothenburg.

After a few days looking at the Saab Aerospace factory and eating a lot of magnificent Swedish fish and drinking gallons of beer, we were flown to Munich to pick up the cars. We drove pedal-to-the-metal along the autobahn into Austria, then a day later on to Switzerland and finally down the Julier Pass with all its serpentine turns, into Italy and on to Monza, where we were to see the cars in action on the circuit in the European touring car championship. There was so much to absorb and it was pretty exciting. I was not a professional driver but I knew how to handle a vehicle (well, maybe not a Mini on the Lachlan Valley Way) so it was all about taking it a piece at a time. What is most interesting is that I remember nearly all of the details of the trip. Memory of that occasion is as sharp as could be. Perhaps it was the overwhelming sense of being involved in something much bigger than just a car. Or the simple act of driving a car. Or the very attractive Volvo public relations department people.

When I returned, there was no expectation that I would write anything, not at least from Volvo. I never did try to work out the cost per person or overall, and how much value there was going to be from the motoring press. I wrote two pieces, both from my sickbed because as soon as I got back I came down with an almighty dose of influenza. What influence they had on Volvo sales in Australia was neither here nor there for me. What was best was driving around the circuit at Monza with one of the Swedish race drivers in the fully race-tuned Volvo, speeding down the straight at 320 kilometres an hour, hitting the chicane and on the damp surface feeling nothing as the car spun through 540 degrees. The driver looked over at me, grinning through his full-face helmet. 'Hey, de track she is a bit wet, yar?' he said as he handbraked it back in line and took off on another lap or two. That was the year that Peter Brock and Allan Moffat contested the race in their '05 Commodore. An Australian they called an independent – Alan Grice – also contested in Chickadee. The Australian motoring writers seemed to spend a lot of time talking to Grice, Moffat and Brock. I wondered how Volvo felt about that.

I've veered off again. A few years later, I entered the world of university lecturing. It's called lecturing but in reality you talk to yourself because the majority of those people called students don't give a toss about what you're saying. Some do. The masters students I taught were mostly full-time workers looking to advance their standing. They were good to be with. I spent a year in the United States at one point, six months at Temple University in Philadelphia then another six at the University of North Carolina in Charlotte. What I wanted to add to this sketch was the difference in travel between academia and the private sector. My trips as a journalist were memorable because they were focused on something. The academic trips, to conferences in every imaginable place in the world, were generally boring and a distraction simply because academics are boring. They are boring when they lecture and they are equally boring when they are away. Although most of them pretend not to be sharing beds with their colleagues' wives or husbands, they do. Not one of those trips was memorable with the exception of two weeks I spent at the United Nations in New York one summer followed by a week at a conference in Porto Allegro in Brazil. The stand out in Brazil was the three lecturers from the University of Loughborough who pretended to know their topic. They blustered and bullshitted to the point where, when we were having a quiet ale one night (they were experts at drinking), I called them out. And to my horror, they agreed they didn't know squat about the topic, but they wanted to come to Brazil. I saw them again some years later in Japan and nothing had changed. Except they drank more and one had cut his hair short. That much I remember.

Dreams & Fantasies

Remember that old bloke who used to shuffle out of his front yard, amble down towards your house and stop out the front, a cigarette shaking away in his hand as he smiled and watched you doing something or other in your garage? Let's call him Keith. Keith didn't say much. Wasn't a big talker, although you got the feeling he may have been a better communicator in his younger days. He turned up pretty regularly on weekends. Stood near the gate until you saw him, then wandered in and watched. He never gave advice, simply watched. Or, now you're closer to the age he must have been then, you suspect he was not only watching, he was dreaming. Perhaps fantasising that he would once more slide under the car and change the oil. Or rebuild the dwarf wall. Or or or.

Keith didn't do anything around his own house. His wife, daughter and granddaughter wouldn't let him. And cancel culture got to him early; he was for his entire career a forester. No, not a model of Subaru, a real deal bloke who looked after and managed forests. Much like those indigenous folk who like to tell everyone who will listen that they managed the Australian bush by a policy of scorched earth. Keith lived long enough not to be able to talk about or even reveal his true working identity for fear of judgement. Saying you were a forester would elicit two reactions; one would be 'I don't know what that is' (think Millennial) the other would be shock and horror, you destroyed the wildlife and the rainforests. So Keith wandered back and forth, smoking, looking lost. Was he fantasising about stuff? Was he dreaming about what the future might still hold or had he grasped that there was nothing more than a vast space to be filled by ambling a hundred metres either side of his drive?

When he died, his wife and daughter and granddaughter packed up, sold the house and left. Straight away. No messing around being despondent, and no ritual performances. No mourners at the funeral. Didn't tell anyone. Keith would have liked a ritual funeral. He was a Freemason and very well instructed in his work.

More importantly, did he dream or fantasise in old age? Did he think about what the future might still hold? Did he prepare himself for a future sexual encounter? Did he shave his genitals and keep himself looking smart in case he came upon someone who might wish for a playful dalliance? An unlikely probability but, nonetheless, something worth considering. Perhaps he fantasised about his widowed sister-in-law. He may have had all sorts of thoughts about her turning up at his house when his wife was out, or of her asking him to come to her place to fix something and on arrival finding her on a hot summer's day lying naked on the lawn chair by the pool, asking him to rub oil all over her saggy baggy body. Or arriving to see her swimming naked in the pool, and while he watches she swims to the steps and gets out standing nude in front of him, her breasts sagging but still, from his viewpoint, looking pretty bloody good. And in his mind she makes no move towards covering herself with a towel; instead she slips his T-shirt over his head, unzips his shorts and goes down on him. Now Keith being in his mid-seventies, this is probably a nice fantasy but a fantasy it shall remain. Even if it were realised, he has not got it up for the past few years and even when he gives himself the occasional tug, it is not without a lot of effort and even then he is more inclined to turn over and go back to sleep than follow through. He might fantasise about what he would do for her despite the lack of erectile encouragement. Perhaps his fingers could do the talking.

After a while, Keith has thought through all the scenarios. He likes to think there is still a possibility that it might happen. Or, as he wanders the street, that there could be someone else. The Chinese woman across the road, for instance. She's not too attractive but then, as he sees himself in the mirror each morning when he shaves, neither is Keith. She might have a few jumps left in her, he thinks, as he watches her drive away, a nod in her direction not reciprocated. Is there any thought in Keith's mind that these fantasies, these dreams of a future Keith, will ever be realised? No. But what if he took them and considered them and rejected them outright rather than having them linger in some anticipatory world where he is no longer in his seventies, no longer suffering from erectile dysfunction? Would Keith feel better if he confronted his fantasies? If he said to himself, look, this or that is never going to happen, so stop thinking about it. Stop it. I suggest Keith would be even more dismal than he appeared to be when he stopped to watch you working on something.

He had nothing to live for other than his fantasies or his dreams. We will never know what his dreams may have been. Maybe he had no fantasy of fucking his sister-in-law. He had no dream of one day taking his gear and walking across Scotland, staying in B&Bs and meeting up with other people his own age, sharing a glass of wine and a stimulating conversation before taking to the footpath the following day. On the other hand, he may have dreamed of getting away from his wife, being admitted to a nursing home where he could be bathed each day by a delightful Polynesian to whom he could jibber without fear of retribution.

My father-in-law, after his wife died, spent six or so years talking about a previous girlfriend, whom he had thrown over sixty-five years earlier when he met the girl who became his wife. He fantasised regularly about what might have been if he had married 'Audrey'. Most of his fantasies involved having sons instead of daughters, which must have been joyful news for his three girls. Audrey, he pronounced, would probably have given him the sons he had spent sixty-odd years yearning for. Well, it was not to be and his dreams and fantasies died with him, as they did with Keith. The difference is that we did not know what Keith dreamed or what fantasies occupied his time. Sadly. Perhaps it was your fault. You ought to have asked Keith what he was thinking, what he wanted in his future. Would he have told you? Most likely not but you'll never know.

The problem with dreams and fantasies is that they take up a lot of time, which is a commodity a seventy-year-old no longer has much of. Rather than take time fantasising about having sex with your sister-in-law, how about you have a rethink? It's never gonna happen, as they say, dude. Many of us have sisters-in-law. Whether they are widowed or not is irrelevant. Keith may have talked briefly about his widowed sister-in-law in the abstract. As if it were something she had created – widowhood – to satisfy a need. Therefore, his desire or fantasy that he would get together with her was nothing more than a layer he applied to the original thought that she had engineered her widowhood for her own advantage. If that were true, then Keith was able to add the extra layer in the desire that he would be the one to satisfy her wants and needs. He probably had extra fantasies that his own wife would fall off the twig to leave him free to exercise his wish. But it was only that. A wish.

The point of dreams and fantasies is not to build layers of reason that something will or will not transpire. All it takes is for the dreamer to act and the desire will be fulfilled. Such thinking is dangerous and leads to all sorts of chaotic behaviour, not least of which is a man who thinks he is desirable to a woman. If he thinks he is desirable, then it stands to reason, in his mind, that all women think him desirable. How wrong he would be. He may put out signals and there may be signifiers, or outliers that he sees as markers which he thinks are there to enable him. Most times, however, he misreads the signs and signals. This is a signal error of judgement. But it needs more than the question and a yes/no answer for it to be acceptable. Remember the old jokes that seemed acceptable at the time? The one where a bloke sees a good-lookin' sheila, sidles up and says in his best exotic voice, 'I suppose a root's out of the question?' The reply was usually, 'Rack off, ya drongo,' and that was that. Boy knew where he stood. Girl knew where he stood. Imagine using that as a pick-up line today. Leave aside the possibility that Millennials don't know a root from a legume, the context, they would say, was disgusting, enough to make you outraged. But it did have its advantages, so I'm told. There was no time-wasting on drinks and dinner, or coffee and cake if you were a tight arse. You knew where you stood and if it was a knock-back, you could move right on. Now, who knows where you might end up? In court perhaps? Although it's okay for some to use similar pick-up lines. A well-known member of parliament while in Sydney on a visit was touring a facility when she turned to her host and said, 'What's a girl got to do to get a root around here?' She was, as they say, barking her knuckles on the wrong concrete. 'I'm not sure I'm the right person to ask,' came the reply. 'I'm gay, you see.' Right time. Wrong place.

Music & Sex

Let's get these out of the way together as they appear to have gone walkabout at around the same time. You may have been happily married for many years. Too many to remember and, aside from a few events that were less than pleasant, they have been good years spent with a woman who has become your best friend. Perhaps that's where the problem lies. They say use it or lose it and, for a lot of seventy-year-olds, things may have begun to drop off in the 'use it' department. There might be a number of reasons, some related to medical problems or others that seem to have created mental blocks. The mental blocks then expand so that if there was ever an opportunity, there were other reasons not to, like being too tired at night. You may be an early riser, so mornings are a good time. But good times for one don't necessarily coincide with good times for the other, who may like to stay sound asleep for as long as possible.

I have a very good mate who, after ten years alone, had begun a new relationship. He reckoned the sex was brilliant (he's sixty-six and she's sixty-one) so maybe it's the younger woman thing. Although sixty-one can only look young if you're staring at it from where he is, and that's approaching seventy. When I go to his place, he still has music playing in the background which is very pleasant and reminiscent of things past. He plays his 60s and 70s stuff and it actually sounds pretty good. Perhaps music and love are meant to be together.

So what happens to stop the music? For some of us, it may have been very sudden. You no longer had any desire to listen to any voices singing at you. Especially those old rockers who sounded spectacular all those years ago. You tried some instrumental music. Some jazz. Classical. But listening to classical pieces over and over makes the house feel like one of those crafty-olde-worlde-wares shops that have a bell over the front door and smell like lavender. I trained as a musician at an early age, learning piano then guitar from fourteen. I have until a few years ago played all my life, sometimes in public and more often in my own company. When I was younger, I could sit in my room with my old guitar and play and sing for hours. In 1978 in San Francisco, I invested all I had in a Martin D35, then again in Philadelphia in 2009 when I had a bit more, I bought a Gretsch Tennessee Rose. Now they sit idle in corners and under beds. Twenty years ago, before I turned fifty, I had the notion to learn cello. I bought one. Tried to play it. Didn't try real hard. Other things got in the way. It sits quietly and sadly now gathering dust. I tell myself I'll give it another go one day but, as another mate pointed out recently, life appears to be slipping away at an accelerating pace.

It's not so much the slipping away, it's more about what can and can no longer be done. A few years ago, I went rock climbing with my son. He's a fine, strong climber, far better than I ever was when I climbed in the 1970s. He took me up an easy climb, a grade eight or nine, and halfway I got a bit shaky and reached too far for a handhold and tore my rotator cuff. You would probably not be surprised to know that every second bloke you speak to has the same problem. Fortunately for me, it was my right shoulder. I'm left-handed, and that in itself is hard to deal with, as left-handedness before the invention of modern writing technology meant ink stains and very poor writing skills. Less fortunate was the fact that the injury made it almost impossible to strum the guitar because the shoulder needed to be splayed outwards at an abnormal angle. After a few minutes playing, it ached, so that meant sticking the instrument back in its case. It's improved since then and the Gretsch has a narrower body, so it's easier to hold and strum but – and there always seems to be a but – it's a hard guitar to set up so that it sounds right. It has a tremolo arm to which the strings attach and getting in the right frame of mind to change the strings or to set it up becomes a matter of whether or not I can be bothered. It all seems too hard until it's done.

Which brings us back to sex. In this case, it doesn't seem too hard, because it's not. We'll talk about prostate and other problems in the physical well-being part. For now, let's say that there seems to be a direct link between an enlarged prostate and the ability to get an erection. So if you have an enlarged prostate – and if you've made it to seventy then you most definitely have one – the chances are you also suffer from what they quaintly call erectile dysfunction. Erectile dysfunction means you can't get it up. And you can't get it up not only when the opportunity to have sex with a woman arises, you actually can't get it up at all. My father had a weird expression – 'a dead bird doesn't fall out of the nest'. I didn't know what he was talking about when I was younger and really didn't care but now I get it.

There are probably things that you can do, or have your partner do for you, but in the end, let's face it, it's really not the same as a good root. All it makes you feel is inadequate anyway, so it's usually best to turn over and go to sleep. At the heart of the matter is whether or not you still think about sex. As blokes, we think about it most of the time. Or we thought about it most of the time before it was pushed to the back of the mind and other more important things took over. The question is why did we stop thinking about it when for so long it had been top of mind? There are some blokes who will say they still think about it all the time. My sixty-six-year-old mate does. But he's not yet seventy. Give him a few years. I met an old bloke in Philadelphia some years ago and he was over seventy then. His wife had died a few years earlier but he still talked about how they had sex every day until she died. Perhaps it killed her. Or she died so she could get away from it. Anyway, he said he would keep doing it until he couldn't. He actually said, 'When that goes, I'm outa here,' which I took to mean when he was no longer physically able he would kill himself.

Relationships

Men, they say, are not good at forming and sustaining relationships with anyone other than men. And dogs. This leaves us pretty much bereft of friendships with women, children, young adults either male or female, or zombies. Leaving aside zombies, we are stereotyped as being unable to form friendships with women because we only see them as sex objects. Children, meanwhile, unless they are our own or our grandchildren, are off limits because every man is inherently a pedophile. When men are framed as predators, there is little room to form relationships, which is why the feminist term 'toxic masculinity' has gained in currency. If men and the image of men can be proscribed by such negative sentiments, then they are limited in their capacity to form relationships with anyone. Another aspect of this is the married man who may wish to be friends with a woman who is not his wife. This is something that is easier to do as we age but for younger men it is an impossibility. Actually, for us it is also impossible. Imagine you wake up one morning and say to your wife, 'I'm heading off to the shops with Wendy this morning then we're going to have lunch. See you later in the day.' Yeah, right.

English writer C.S. Lewis believed friendship arose out of companionship when two or more of the companions discovered that they had in common some insight or interest which the others did not share and which, till that moment, each believed to be his own unique treasure. There are more than five million people in Sydney, the city in which I live. There are approximately twenty whom I know well enough to call friends, which means there are 4,999,980 I don't know or who, in Lewis's definition, are companions only. As we age, we become less interested in forming new friendships while many of the old ones fall away, or simply become unused to the point of neglect. Our position is not at all satisfying. Which is why there is a need for a service such as Lifeline. While Lifeline is primarily about diminishing the rate of national suicide, it is also a first contact point for the lonely and alone.

Twenty-four-hour crisis supporters provide not only suicide prevention services, they also have conversations about mental health support and emotional assistance. Lifeline's website states in bold language that 'You are not alone. We're here to listen.' Lifeline's crisis support telephones receive a call every thirty seconds and each year more than one million people ask for its support. As far as suicide statistics go, every day nine people kill themselves and six of them are men. That's more than 2,000 men's lives lost every year. While depression is claimed as a major factor, the historical image of men as being unable to form relationships, and their inability to show emotion or empathy, contribute to depression which in turn leads to suicidal ideation. Male suicide numbers vary from country to country. Figures are provided by 100,000 of population, with Antigua having no suicides per 100,000 to Lesotho having 146 per 100,000. Male suicides calculated by the World Health Organisation are Australia 17; USA 22; Canada 15; New Zealand 15; Britain 10; Russia 38. In the past twenty years in Australia, the rate of men succeeding has remained relatively stable; in 2000 the number was 18.8. It decreased by 2010 to 15.9 and gradually rose again to 17 by 2020. In contrast, Britain's rate dropped from 12 to 10.4, while in the USA the rate rose from 16.4 to 22.4. New Zealand's rate dropped from 20.8 to 15.4, while Lesotho, a country surrounded by South Africa, went from 74 in 2000 to 146 twenty years later.

Not all older men who suffer depression will act on suicidal thoughts. Many live isolated lives, sometimes after the death of a long-term relationship with a wife or partner, and sometimes they live their lives as single men. Much as being alone can cause men to become depressed, so too isolation can create feelings of loneliness. It's all very well to live in a city of five million but when you are alone in that space, things look very different. You may be alone, which means you are in a state of being by yourself, and this may not be how you wish it to be. Many callers to Lifeline, known as help seekers, make the call not because they are alone, but because they are suffering from loneliness. To be lonely is an emotional state rather than a physical state such as being alone. To be lonely is to suffer a feeling of being disconnected or a feeling of loss. For older men, it can occur when family move away or when grown children move out of home leaving a man either with a wife or alone. Loneliness can surface when a regular connection is broken. Men generally manage well after the loss of their wife. They have the experience of age and there was always the certainty that death would come to one of them, which meant they could prepare emotionally and spiritually. There is no such things as sudden death. And yet all death is sudden given that one moment one is alive and breathing and the next not.

Forty years ago, author Philippe Ariès wrote *The Hour of Our Death*, a book which examines death and its permutations through the centuries. It is the title, however, which is important to us here. As we age, we get time to contemplate death; we are allowed to think about it in more detail and when the last hour arrives, we can take the time to embrace it. But that is not much help in understanding why relationships sustain us, why we develop long-term relationships and why we feel lonely when they cease to exist.

Loneliness and depression are hard to drive out. Depression can happen even when one has a loving and caring relationship. Older men get sad about all manner of things but it does not necessarily lead to depression. Quite often it is because no one is interested in our opinions or our ideas. Stereotype and image come in to play here. If we are looked at, which is not often, we are evaluated and judged and the result is not pretty. Our opinions don't count. What we say is sexist and misogynistic. We are consigned not to history but to nothingness. We exist physically but the evaluation of our mental capacity by others is that there is nothing worthwhile there. Even family members shrug us off with 'oh, boomer' or 'oh, granddad'. Sons, who are supposed to see us in their own image, are as bad as daughters when it comes to sloughing us off. Some show a degree of tact, others less so. The roll of the eyes and the snort are all that are needed to shut us down. After enough rolls and snorts, it becomes easier to say nothing and to have no opinion. Unless you want to spend the next few days or week getting the silent treatment. Thus, loneliness can be found in many different quarters. The question is how to deal with it. How not to become sad or melancholy.

Dating Sites & Apps

So you want to get out a bit more, go on a date, or, heaven forbid, think about a 'sexual encounter' with a woman. A Canadian researcher Peggy Klienplatz believes intimacy improves the older we get. She did some research into the sex lives of sixty- to eighty-year-olds that showed people were actually having sex. Oh my goodness. What a discovery. This prompted an America, Stacy Lindau, to study the sexual behaviour of grown-ups. She got funding to show that half of the people aged between sixty-five and seventy-four had got a root at least once in the year of the study. Crikey. I had to reread that figure. Once? Yes. Once. Seems like a low number. Dr Lindau found herself on the precipice of an even bigger discovery. When she spoke with her 'patients' they revealed that 'dating apps' had become more popular and provided the impetus that had not been available in the past. Well, whacko. I think I might want a bit of a refund if I spent money on a dating app and got a once-a-year return. Let's look at some of the sites, the costs and who in Australia the users might be.

A quick Duck Duck Go search with the words 'dating sites for seventy-year-olds' reveals the top five are zoosk, eharmony, elite, silver, and match. Note the lack of capital letters. Probably too much to ask a senior to hold down caps while typing. Tinder and Bumble appear to be the leading sites. There is another one called academic singles, which offers you the chance to find your perfect partner with a similar educational background. It guarantees time and money saving with a higher chance of meeting your perfect match. How rude. The site gives you the opportunity to look for a man or a woman. Then there's one called flirt, where you can also look for both but, if you're over seventy-eight, bad luck, bro, there's no age group on there for you. Another one called benaughty has the same images and click boxes as flirt. And it too stops at seventy-eight. Silversingles promises that love doesn't stop at a certain age and just like happiness it matures as it grows like a fine wine that definitely gets better with age. This site offers its services completely free unless you want to invest in finding a partner. Then there is a premium option. How much do these things actually cost?

Most of the sites are free to join but then they start costing money when you begin looking. They range between $30 and $200 a month. The real questions are not about whether you should take the plunge, the real questions are what you might be getting yourself into and what might be the outcome if you do. The sites themselves are pretty keen to pump up their own tyres and to have you leap on board so you anticipate a smooth ride. They claim to have millions of users but how many of those users have actually been successful in finding something they think they are looking for? Our favourite for obvious reasons is Plenty of Fish. As with most sites, you enter details so you can meet other fifty-plus singles near you. You identify as man seeking woman, woman seeking man, man seeking man or woman seeking woman. Next it becomes more transactional as you enter your postcode and your date of birth. But what if you put a fake birthdate? To get any further into the site, you need to add an email address so that's as far as we went with it.

We asked a few survey questions of our own. One mate found what was billed as a perfect partner. It turned out she lived a long, long way from where he lived and she expected him to spend weekends at her place. He had family commitments but she became a bit possessive and even aggressive in the sex department. She was a good nine years younger than him and still had a few jumps left in her, which, to his credit, he tried to keep up with. It was the dawn-buster that got him in the end. Didn't mind a couple of goes in the evening but having to front up again at sparrows' was not quite how he saw it. He decided to call it quits but she was not ready, saying that he would miss the sex. He agreed but added that the need to use the little blue diamond to enhance the performance became a bit monotonous. He's a bit reluctant about hopping back in to the pool. Likes spending time with his grandkids and being free to do what he wants when he wants. And the sex? If he finds someone sometime later, all well and good but for the time being he's happy to go solo.

Another mate was a bit more persevering despite the match-ups not being real good. They looked good on paper, he said, but after a few months they all tell him he's got serious problems and should see a therapist. His problem is not that he needs a therapist. His problem is that he is too nice a bloke – a good egg – and he manages to find some of the wackiest women imaginable. They spend a few months drinking and eating their way through his wallet, let him take them places and pay for everything, then get bored. Like the earlier mate, he wants to spend time with his family (both of them are long-time divorced) and the women he hooks up with want to monopolise him. He does a bit of compartmentalising – tries to keep events and activities separate; does stuff with his adult kids and other times does stuff with the new woman. For both of these men, there has been a constant, not of ex-wives, but that they have rebuilt their lives since their divorces and have become relatively financial at a time in life when they can't afford to be taken again to the cleaners. So this plays on their minds when they form new relationships. And their 'kidults' are always in the background keeping a watchful eye on the future inheritance.

The question is, what is it that draws older men to dating sites? Is it that they have no other way of meeting women? Similarly, one might question why they wish to meet a woman with whom to develop a relationship. I know a few men, widowers, who have made no attempt to find and develop a new relationship. That doesn't mean they don't wish to have a new relationship. Most often it has to do with their love for their wives which continues passed death. They are often lonely but not lonely enough to become involved in the transactional commercialisation of dating.

As older men, we have seen too many things and had too many experiences to allow ourselves to be algorithmed into new relationships. If you ask a search engine to describe a dating site, it pops up innumerable examples of how to write a profile of yourself. Write a profile? Bloody buggery. There appears to be no limit to the degree of deception you might wish to include; how to write an unstoppable senior dating profile; leave a little mystery; follow the 70:30 rule (whatever that is); pretend to be a scuba diver, mountaineer, race car driver and olympic skier all at once. This is partly a sad indictment of the world we find ourselves inhabiting; where there are fewer places we as older men can feel comfortable and unthreatened. We are overwhelmed with advertising products and services that are designed to enhance our already receding lives; why add to the confusion and anxiety by telling us we must have impact or be impactful, find a new partner and get on with the joy of living? The pressure is enormous. Unless we refrain from going anywhere near social media and its dating app offspring. Stay away from it altogether. Save your money and your sanity. Life is too short to waste. As Greek philosopher Aristotle remarked, perfect friendships subsist between those who are good and whose similarity consists in their goodness: for these men wish one another's good in similar ways.

Mates

For Aristotle, friendship was an essential component of living a good life. In other words, mates are critical to your well-being. And while you may not think so, you are as important to their well-being. There are all types of mates: good mates, bad mates, mates you drink with, mates you play golf with, mates you play bowls with, mates you fish with. I have different mates for different occasions. By that I don't mean I compartmentalise mates. Some of them overlap. I play golf with one and we also bowl together. We have a few ales together after bowls and golf but we don't socialise much at other times. I have a mate I fish with but he doesn't play golf or bowl or do anything else but fish. He's a damn good fisherman, which is what he is. I refuse to refer to him as a fisher. He might be an angler but generally speaking he is a fisherman. And 'fishermen will aye ga'eng oot as lang as fish swim in the sea'. Or so they once sang. I have a mate with whom I bushwalk and cycle. We became bushwalking mates by accident. We played golf together, then we started talking about walking and before long we were off on day trips. Most of them required that we could access the walk from a railway station (yes, railway station, not train station – Millennials can call it a train station but for any seventy-year-old it will remain a station on a railway and the train will travel on the railway with other rolling stock). And there had to be a pub nearby. Blackheath in the Blue Mountains became a favourite, as did the Gardner's Inn and its cider on tap. Trouble is, trains these days don't have toilets.

I have other mates who have been around a long time. A couple of them I've known for more than forty years. We don't see each other as much as we used to but nothing changes when we do. We pick up where we left off and continue the conversation or whatever it was that was going on.

Then there are family mates. It's not as stupid as it sounds. You can be mates with your family members, your sons, or your sons-in-law if you have any of them, or your daughters. I have a mate who is one of the best. He is my wife's cousin, so I only met him through being married to her. But when my house was burgled and ransacked, he was the first person I thought of to call. And he dropped what he was doing and made sure the place was secure while I drove the six hours back from where I was after I had been alerted to the problem by a neighbour.

Meanwhile, some blokes pretend to be mates, then, when they've had enough, they cut you off. There was one bloke who did that (and to be truthful, I've probably done it too, though I can't recall any specifically). I played golf with him for years then one day out of the blue he rang and said he wasn't playing with me any more because I was too unreliable. Turns out I had pulled out of a club round which I told him about but then he put his name in with three Millennials who did the dirty on him and played at another time. When tee-time arrived, he was left standing like a shag on a rock, so he blamed me. That was the end of the friendship. It was, in Aristotle's terms, a friendship of utility. When it was of no use, it was lost. I recall years ago, being bemused when I overheard someone say 'he is a personal friend'. This plays up the Aristotelian notion of 'philia' being of three kinds; pleasure, utility and virtue. A personal friend to this man was different to a business friend. He may have trusted his business friend, so there was utility and some degree of financial pleasure but no virtue.

Mates are those blokes you see when you see them. You look out for each other when necessary. You trust each other. There has got to be a lot of trust. That's what makes you mates. That's why you don't always stay mates with blokes you work with over the years. At work, you get thrown together because you have mutual skills or abilities but that rarely translates into long-term mateship. At seventy, you don't need a whole lot of mates. And you've pretty much done with work. That was another planet on which you no longer reside. As long as you didn't work so hard and focus so much on work that you now find yourself alone with no mates. That can happen. One of the reasons it happens is that you made it to three score and ten but your mates fell off the twig somewhere along the way. Dead mates are still mates. You may not be able to play golf with them but they are still there with you. You don't have to discard them. Go and visit them every now and then. Tell them what's been going on.

I remember my father had a mate. They had gone to school together and they were still there at the end. It was an almost indescribable relationship. It was mateship at its best. It was something that probably died with them. If I tried to describe it, it would be like this. They grew up in a small town. One was Catholic, one was Methodist. In those days, there was plenty of bigotry around, as there is still. In midlife, my father would rail against Catholics and against the Labor Party, although he never revealed his voting preferences, saying it was a secret ballot and therefore one of the few things that a man had for himself. He may have been opposed to Catholicism and Labor but his best mate was Catholic. I suspect his mate Jack was also not greatly interested in Methodism or Protestantism but he never revealed it.

They had grown up in a small town and they had gone off to war when they were in their early twenties. That experience, though they were in different battalions in different countries, strengthened their mateship through their involvement with the RSL, the Returned Services League of Australia. Saturday afternoon in summer was hot and steamy but they passed the middies of Blue Bow lemonade out of the window to the young fellas practising in the cricket nets at the side of the 'Razzle'.

I have a perpetual image of Jack standing at the window, side-on so he could continue talking to his mates, schooner of Resch's in hand, offering bowling advice as we blazed away under the midday sun following our morning match at some local cricket ground or other. My father drove me to cricket when I was younger but in later years at high school it was pedal-to-the-metal on the fixed wheeler a couple of miles into town. (Sadly, when Jack died, his wife remarked that he would never have won a father of the year award. He had three daughters.)

Mates in those days helped each other build their houses and their sheds, and took time off from work to do other jobs for mates in need. Towns were like that. I can't speak for cities or suburbs because I didn't spend my early years in them. I remember my father taking three weeks off work (he was a public servant with a state government department in the city and commuted by train every day of his forty-five-year working life). He took over a local garage, where he wore a boiler suit, dispensed fuel and booked in vehicles for repairs. It was such a change from his day job. My image is of him in the apron of the garage filling a tank in his grease-stained overalls. It was his brother-in-law he was doing it for. He was a rep for the petrol company and the service station owner had got sick. My father's brother-in-law asked him and he did it. That's what mates did.

Fathers & Sons

We all have fathers. Some of us have them longer than others, meaning that some live longer. We might have a father for sixty years but it would be rare for a seventy-year-old to still have his father. Men have a habit of dying young, so many boys live most of their lives without the benefit of a father – his presence or his influence. Fathers, whether we like it or not, shape their sons as they make their way towards becoming men. Even in older age, the influence of the father is still there. It may not be a good influence but it is still there. Secular society and 'woke' Millennials have for many years been actively working to destroy the image of men, beginning with the image of God, and Jesus Christ as the son of God. The campaign has been effective; you only need to look at the numbers of worshippers in any church on any Sunday to see that the generations since World War II show very little interest in God. Congregants are mostly older women and not because their husbands or partners have died. Men generally have abandoned Christianity. It's a different story for Islam, where men worship regularly at mosques and during the day wherever they are at the time they are called to prayer. I recall some years ago seeing a taxi driver pull off the main road into the gates of a private Christian boys' school, take out his prayer mat, kneel on a grassed area and proceed to pray.

Fathers have more influence over their sons than they can ever know.

Despite the attempts by educators to redirect the mind of the boy, the father – or the father figure if there is no father – will inexorably shape the thinking and therefore the actions of most boys. By this, I mean that boys today, if they attend government primary and high schools, will rarely have the benefit of a male teacher. In the classroom where women prevail, the boy is a second-class citizen. But when he has the benefit of a father, then he has the benefit of balance, of becoming a man rather than being constantly told he is part of the problem.

Men, particularly older men, are not good at talking. They may argue about their footy tipping and they're quick to tell you why they hate certain politicians but when it comes to talking about the issues that are really important to them, such as their prostate problem, or their relationship problem, or their financial problem, the canvas is blank. Men do not know how to talk about personal issues because they have no training. They are told from an early age to grow up and be a man, don't cry like a girl, don't be a baby. There are a lot of external pressures applied to men simply because they are men, which makes it very difficult to navigate through life and remain a man. It is why men don't talk. Whatever they say is misinterpreted, argued against or called out as being wrong, so what's the point in saying anything in the first place.

I had conversations with two men which were on the same day but almost polar opposites. The first was with a sixty-nine-year-old who said he was in so much physical pain he could barely think. He had a number of ailments that caused the pain and on a good day the best he could hope for was to sit on his back veranda and look at the trees in his backyard and hope that birds flew in so that he had something to focus on. He said his medico had recommended numerous drugs but the pain was so constant and intense that he would have needed a handful every few hours but that taking so many gave him all sorts of other side effects. Some natural remedies eased things a little but generally all he wanted to do was to stay alive for the next few weeks until he turned seventy; then, he said, he would make preparations to kill himself. There was no one to support him. He said his wife of many years didn't want to know and was sick of listening to him. He said all he wanted was to have a conversation so that he could think about something else for half an hour or so and not think about the pain. He didn't want to talk politics or sport or to get angry with his wife. He simply wanted someone to listen to how he felt about God.

The second conversation was with a man in his late twenties. He was a big bloke with a bald head, tattoos on his face, neck, arms and head, a neat ziff and a black T-shirt with black shorts. Essentially someone you would feel uncomfortable meeting on a dark night. He was my barber. While he was working on what's left of my hair, he asked me if I lived in the town. I said I lived close by but had been doing a Lifeline shift. He thought I said I had called Lifeline and he immediately got agitated and concerned. We clarified the situation, which led to him revealing he had suffered from anxiety and depression and that he still lay awake each night worrying about something he could not explain. What emerged was that he was not in fear of anything. He was a huge bloke and I suspected he was very strong. What he had was dread. He dreaded something but he didn't know what – somewhere in the future that might involve him, or it might involve his kids and his wife. It may not have had much to do with his present feelings but it turned out that he had a pretty bad childhood. His father, he said, was an ice addict. We had been talking about the fact that a lot of men in their thirties have easy access to ice, or methamphetamines, which they think they can control but aside from the physical and mental toll, the financial toll is what beats them. Anyway, he said his old man was a dick because he hadn't cared about anyone except himself and he went around breaking entering and stealing to sell whatever he stole to get more ice.

My barber, the big bloke with the tats and shaved head, was revealing to me something that had affected him deeply and that possibly remained with him and was the cause of his depression and dread. The point of this anecdote is that in neither of the conversations were we looking for answers. The point was that we were talking. Whether it had value for either of them is unknown. It had value for me because in the first it gave a clearer sense of self. It was not about being better off because I have no pain, at least at present – there have been some doozies – it was about connecting with another man who said at the end of the conversation that he felt better even if only for half an hour. In the second example, my barber felt comfortable enough to connect with an older man – actually older than his grandpop – and to share some of his experiences with someone he may not usually come in contact with. For me, this was the whole point, even though the discount on the haircut was a bit of a bonus. Both men were the real deal.

The sixty-nine-year-old had almost completed his three score and ten, a significant phrase for him which resonated when I used it in the conversation. He had experienced stuff you would not wish on your worst enemy yet he continued to live and act as a man is expected to live and act. The younger man, the barber, I observed was very comfortable among his peers; a couple of middle-eastern men of similar age and a Pacific islander of the same size and strength. His work environment was real, there were a lot of hood shakes, and yet he was just as comfortable moving out of it to discuss his emotional state with someone he had never met before.

Part of the reason men call telephone services such as Lifeline and Mensline is that they can talk to someone anonymous who will listen without judgement or recommendation. They are not all suicidal or having suicidal thoughts. They simply want someone, preferably another man, to listen to what they have to say and to acknowledge their existence. A lot of time is spent these days in a number of countries, but particularly those which were colonised a few centuries ago, in acknowledging the existence of indigenous men and women. It is a positive step but it has a negative impact on non-indigenous men whose contribution to society is no longer seen as important or relevant. In fact, there are some who attempt to demean the work of generations of men. Our fathers and our fathers' fathers had no way of knowing that their sons were to be discriminated against because they were men. Had they foreseen such an abominable situation, would they have been able to forestall or contain it? Probably not. It would have been unimaginable as they consciously or unconsciously skilled and educated their sons.

Well-being

The *Shorter Oxford English Dictionary* defines well-being (yes, hyphenated) under a subheading of 'Well' as healthy, contented, or prosperous condition; moral or physical welfare (of a person or community ; satisfactory condition (of a thing). It sits among a variety of other usages such as well-away, well-adjusted, well-built, well-defined, well-earned, well-padded, well-spaced, well-travelled, well-worn. all the way to well-wrought.

Our well-being is not something to be taken lightly. As we age, we become less well-tempered but more well-padded. Less well-loved, more well-worn. Less well-adjusted, and less well-behaved. Perhaps that's how others see us. Some ratbags (see later sketch) go out of their way to be annoyingly less well-behaved, which in turn makes them less well-loved. But they are generally bunging on an act that they think is hilarious. We may become less well-loved because our opinions and ideas are considered outdated. Like hyphenating words. It might irritate Millennials, so they love us less because we do something that was once acceptable but is now no longer. They may love us less or think we're not well-adjusted because we can poke big holes in ideologies such as Net Zero 2050.

Generally, by the time you get to seventy, you are a lot of the wells joined together – well-adjusted, well-loved, well-worn, well-behaved, well-travelled, well-fed, well-proportioned and well-mannered. All these wells go together to make the definition of well-being, well, work. Our well-being is up to us. No one else gives a rats whether we are in a healthy, contented or prosperous condition. We might be on the edge of poverty or we might have more money than we know what to do with but only we know that. I know men in their seventies who remain well-groomed so that they give the appearance of being well-off. This is not always the case. They may, however, have a reasonable sense of well-being, as much as the man who has millions in his share and property portfolio.

What is a sense of well-being? Is it actually well-being, or is it how you feel about yourself not in isolation, but within the whole spectrum of our existence? French writer Jean-Paul Sartre viewed the existence of man as being and nothingness, where being causes one to look at one's self as an object as we appear to others. He believed relationships were created by one person's attraction to how the other person made them feel about themselves. On the other hand, he believed we were existing in an overall condition of nothingness, or no thing-ness, so we ought to have free consciousness but we are constrained because we have to make continual conscious choices. Millennials have taken Sartre and applied his idea of self as an object in other people's vision and turned it on its head. They don't wear different clothes for different occasions based on who might judge them; they wear the same crappy T-shirt and jeans to dinner, to the beach, to everywhere. As we get older, though, we tend to polarise what we do. We either don't give a stuff and become like Millennials, wearing the same old kit everywhere, or we're ultra-conscious of what we look like, which shapes our sense of our well-being so we are finicky about how we dress.

I had pressure applied to me from some quarters about buying a new suit for an impending wedding. I have a couple of suits that I no longer wear. They would have been all right on the day. But my well-being told me they looked outdated and the wrong colour so, as I mentioned earlier, I went and looked at new ones that were of lesser quality than my existing ones but a snugger fit, which is the 'look'. I didn't buy a new one. And I didn't wear the old ones. I wore a jacket and a similar coloured pair of pants. I felt okay. My well-being in this instance was shaped by my being conscious that I was not the focus of the event. So it pretty much mattered not a jot what I wore. Some of the thirty-somethings wore mismatched clothes but they were contented because they didn't care what anyone thought of them. The thirty-something women, on the other hand, were suitably conscious and thereby suitably attired.

Another recent example of how we see ourselves and how it affects our well-being occurred in Abu Dhabi. A thirty-something European couple arrived to travel on Etihad Airways. They were told they could not book because the woman was wearing jeans. They were very expensive designer jeans but no luck even though her husband was also wearing jeans. Middle-eastern culture does not look favourably on women poorly dressed by their standards. The woman's well-being was of no account. She may have been well-educated, well-intentioned and well-travelled but she was not allowed on that plane.

Our well-being is directly related to our health and partly to how contented we are with our lives. Health is important. If we're unwell, as I've described elsewhere, all our mental focus will be on how we can become physically well. We'll have no time to worry about how we smell, or if our jammies need washing when we're cooped up in our sick beds. In this, we have no consciousness of our being other than that we are unwell. Our unwell-being takes over our well-being. When we feel physically okay, then our mental well-being is also improved. Mind you, there can be times when mental well-being is not so crash-hot, which in turn leads to a deterioration in physical well-being.

To have mental and physical well-being in balance at seventy takes a bit of doing. Not least when there are a variety of what we might call exogenous variables floating around and bumping in to you, throwing you out of kilter. It's no easy task to maintain a balance between the mental and physical. Part of the answer lies not so much in being active all the time but in how you choose your activities. One of the most boring things in the world is to walk around the block every morning or afternoon either with or without your dog in tow. The same old same old depressing landscape of houses and footpaths and high-rise blocks of flats will be all you have. You can try to make it feel better by telling yourself the exercise is good for you, or you can listen to something or other on your headphones, but at the end of the day it's a bloody boring way to waste time. Even if it is supposed to be good for you.

I know a bloke who is a little older than seventy. In fact, he's closer to eighty and he says he has to go out and do something every day or he will go mad. He lives alone and plays bowls twice a week, golf once and tennis twice. That leaves two days for him to go mad. What does he mean by go mad? Does he mean he's uncomfortable with his own company? He has a dog. He takes the dog for a walk around the block most afternoons. What he means when he says he'll go mad if he doesn't do things is that he's lonely. If he gets out, he sees other people, at the same time as getting some exercise.

Another chap the same age spends his days administering a local small club. He rarely looks contented or prosperous – conditions for well-being – but he says it's better than sitting at home with no one to talk to. So well-being in these examples becomes a function of being with others or being around others rather than being alone.

A great deal has been written about well-being. In 2010, a survey by Gallup provided the impetus for the development of a taxonomy of well-being. Career, social, financial, physical and community were words attached to well-being and 66% of respondents did well in at least one category. The really awful bit was that 7% of people surveyed in 150 countries claimed to be doing well in all five categories. It may be that the remaining 93% take too much notice of all the things we're supposed to do if we want to increase our well-being. There's plenty of advice – don't smoke, eat a balanced diet, be social, get out in the sun, find new hobbies, exercise every day, deal with stress, and sleep well. Good luck with that.

Well-being, according to *Oxford*, is also about the mental and physical welfare of a person or community. Let's take a squizz at community. This is a word that has intrigued me for some time and has been the subject of research, most notably by American Robert Nisbet of Columbia University. Nisbet, who was eighty-three when he died in 1996, lived across a century in which the term community, for a variety of reasons, began to gain currency. His book *The Quest for Community* was first published in 1953. His first three chapters were entitled the loss of community, the image of community and the problem of community. But what is community and what does it mean to us now? We're told by those in the know that we're part of the wider community when it means avoiding Covid-19; of being part of the global community when we're told to fight climate change; and of being part of our local community when we want to feel all warm and fuzzy about something or other.

Let's consult our *Oxford* again. Community, it states, is firstly a body of individuals, and secondly, a quality, or state. For the first, it expands it to being an organised political or social body or a body of people living in the same locality, or a body of nations united by common interests. Secondly, it is defined as a common character, or a sense of common identity; life in association with others, society or the social state. In this, it seems that community has supplanted society as the word of choice for what we do collectively. Ten years in to the twenty-first century, one of Australia's leading advocates for a better society, Tim Costello, formed an organisation known as the Community Council of Australia. It's an independent, non-political member organisation established to enhance charitable and not-for-profit work. The term community is prominent in all its published matter. Its uses include building flourishing communities; the broader Australian community; all our communities; schools and local communities; engaged in the communities they live in; and fundamental value of community. If we use the *Oxford* definition of well-being as the moral or physical welfare of a community, then the work of the CCA is crucial to the future of our society if we take society to mean the aggregate of people living together in a more or less ordered community.

Now all this sounds a bit serious but it's important for us as seventy-year-olds to know where we fit in these communities and in society, so we need to be able to define them for our own well-being. For Bob Nisbet, the contemporary family has been made to carry a 'conscious symbolic importance that is greater than ever, but it does so with a structure much smaller in size and of manifestly diminishing relevance to the larger economic and political ends of contemporary society'. Nisbet wrote this in the midtwentieth century but Tim Costello echoes his remarks now, towards the end of the first quarter of the twenty-first, when he asks what if we could live in a country where incarceration rates are falling, where the suicide rate is less that the road toll and where levels of violence against women and children have been significantly reduced? Nisbet's symbolic family has become Costello's community. And we seventy-year-olds can make valuable contributions to it at all levels. How we do that is up to us.

Food

One of the most valuable books in my small library was published by Lansdowne Press more than thirty years ago. It was written, or compiled might be a better word, by Josephine Rogers, a well-known and well-regarded nutritionist. The book is entitled *What Food Is That & How Healthy Is It?* For me, with a non-alcoholic fatty liver diagnosis some years ago, the contents of the book proved life-redeeming. Ms Rogers provides words and pictures about every conceivable food item. The book is subdivided into sections on meat, vegetables, fruit, grain, pasta, cakes and everything in between including dressings and vinegars, cheese, pulses, fats and oils and salts and baking agents.

Did you know, for example, that celeriac is very low in kilojoules but a good source of dietary fibre and only a moderate source of vitamin C and iron? So why is it so popular? There must be better alternatives. Here's one on the previous page, cassava, which is an excellent source of iron, magnesium, vitamin C and a good source of fibre. Curiously, it makes no mention of quarter-pounders or cheeseburgers. Does this mean the QP or the BigMac are not considered to be food? With age comes wisdom, they say. But the Maccas brekkie when you're on the road or the quarter-pounder meal for lunch is a wonder to behold. Throw in the free 'seniors' coffee when you have a seniors card and life gets no better. Unless, of course, you suffer from any number of ailments that relate to your food intake. Too much sugar – diabetes; too much fat – high cholesterol; too much grog – liver failure.

The list goes on and on until you get to the point where you feel there's nothing you can eat or drink that won't kill you. Part of the problem is that as you get older, it's much easier to work with pre-packaged and pre-cooked meals because it's harder to get to the shop and you can't be bothered cooking every lunchtime and every evening. Better to stick a pre-pack in the microwave or one of those already-made pizzas in the oven for twenty minutes. But there are consequences. You might tell yourself that you're going to do more exercise after every pizza or bowl of ice cream but it never eventuates. When you find yourself in hospital for an angiogram and the specialist tells you he's going to admit you immediately so he can insert arterial stents, then you could be in a lot of trouble. The solution may have been a better diet when you were younger but now, at seventy, it's probably a bit late to be lecturing you on what you ought to have done.

How then, do we come at the problem of food and nutrition for a body that has seen three score and ten years, probably will be lucky to see another decade, and feels like every manufacturer of food products is trying to kill you? One way is to stop worrying about it. Worry causes stress, stress causes anxiety and anxiety can cause depression. When you have depression, or anxiety, or stress, eating well is not a high priority. If we can be less worried about ourselves – about our weight loss or gain, about or levels of exercise – then we're on the right track. When I had a recent blood test, the quack said everything was okay at present but I needed to be vigilant. She quoted back to me that because my father had been diabetic, if I were to gain a lot of weight or to not do any exercise, I too would be a candidate for the diabetes. (When I was a kid, I thought they were saying sugared iabeties. Silly boy.)

But back to the point. I am not going to gain a huge amount of weight, nor am I going to stop doing the physical stuff unless something befalls me that lays me up. And even then, I won't start eating copious quantities of food. The lecture was unnecessary but that seems to be what corporate medicos do these days as a matter of course. Give everyone the same lecture. I know of a number of men and women in their nineties in nursing homes who are constantly badgered by medical and ancillary staff about getting out and walking and having physio and keeping their mental state by attending painting classes where they relearn to colour in between the lines and get gold stars. Bollocks to that. Leave them alone. If they want to sit all day and watch television subtitles and eat ice cream for breakfast and soup for dinner, bloody-well let them. The question, though, is how best to sustain yourself as a seventy-year-old so you get to enjoy the nursing home ice cream and television subtitles. Sustenance is important. I have conversations with a lot of older men and women who are anxious and stressed and depressed. Ninety-five per cent of them reveal that they don't eat breakfast or if they do it consists of a cuppa and not much else.

In the late 1960s to the early 1970s, there was a takeaway located right on the first of the Circular Quay jetties. It was a small space hovering over the water at the entrance to the ferry. They sold sandwiches and other things but the best was the hamburger. And it was the way the Greek behind the counter took your order that made it so exciting. You would stand in a nice orderly line a little way out into the promenade and if there were too many people waiting, which was always the case at five past one on a weekday, then the line took a ninety-degree angle and swept towards the second ferry wharf. When it was your turn, you said in a loud voice, 'a hamburger'. The old Greek, who was probably not very old but he looked old to someone in their twenties, would write it on a note pad, then half turn his head and shoulder towards the large grill and say in a very loud voice, 'One hamburger please thanks', but with a strong Greek or middle-eastern accent. We had no idea what he was except that when he said it, it sounded more like 'Wern hembugga plizz thenx.' You paid him then stepped back or lolled along the railing for a minute or three until he shouted out from the cave, 'Wern hembugga plizz thenx.' It was a simple thing. The tone of voice was the clue. A moderate shout over the shoulder to activate the process, a loud shout out past the other customers to finalise it.

Compare that with the drive-in at the Golden Arches and your present age of around seventy. With the noise from the car exhaust, traffic on the road and other sundry sounds, a little girly voice squeaking out of a not-so-very-loud loudspeaker asking, 'Can I take your order?' when you haven't yet put your foot on the brake let alone looked at the neon menu can be hard to understand. Then you get to go through the rigmarole of selection. Plenty of options that all add up to pretty much the same thing – one hamburger please thanks. And don't even start on the free seniors coffee. Very nice of Maccas to offer a senior coffee free of charge to those with a 'seniors card' but to get it, you frequently have to provide written evidence from a JP or other important person (dentists come into this category; why, I have no idea). All they have to do is poke their little heads out of their cavern and they will see that you're barely holding it together.

Negotiating the drive-through was hard enough. Reaching over to give them your credit card or, shock and horror, cash, makes the hand begin its anticipatory tremors. To then have to produce a seniors card which you've most likely not used in months to show to a teenager to prove your identity is, to put it mildly, not worth the effort of the coffee itself. Sometimes, though, they don't give a rats. You could order six free ones and they'd shove them out with a 'have a nice day'. I was on the far south coast once and my seniors card was not. The little androgynous person would not accept that I was over sixty-five. He/she/they insisted on calling the manager even though I said forget the coffee. The manager came and was not interested in seeing a pension card. He provided a lovely lecture on what a pension card was and how one did not need to be over sixty-five to be on a pension. Here I was, all 365 days times seventy listening to a pre-pubescent poking his entire head and shoulders through the little window. At the end, I said forget the coffee, to which he responded, 'Well, I'll let it go this time and you can have the coffee, but remember to bring it with you next time.' Wern hembugga to him.

Sport

When we were young, we had an enormous choice of games available to us. Games being the correct term rather than sport. Or sports, which now appears to be the accepted plural. We already have fishes, breads and cheeses, so why not sports? What next? Sheeps? It's all a bit confusing when various activities can be cobbled together such as a game of golf, a game of chess or a game of bowls. Then we have a game fishing competition, a game of rugby, a game of cricket, a game of tennis.

So let's stick to games at present. There are a few anomalies. Cycling is one. We don't say a game of cycling. We go cycling. We don't say a game of motor. We watch motorsport. Cycling's an interesting one. Remember back in the 1960s when you had a fixed-wheel Speedwell? One big sprocket and one little sprocket. And no front brake, only a back brake if you had a newer model or when you were younger a back-pedal brake, which meant you had a fixed sprocket which acted as a brake when you hit the pedal hard when it was in horizontal position. None of this fancy multi-sprocket stuff, although a couple of kids from across the river had three-speed with front and back brakes. One of their dads owned the local bike shop. They rode across the bridge and along the highway to school.

Bikes were parked in circular steel contraptions or dropped on the ground in the grass. No locks in those days. No one stole bikes, especially grotty old ones. Mine had a carrier on the back so I could attach my Globite school case. They sell on eBay now for around $100 but anyone who buys them didn't ever have to cart their books and lunch around in one. Mine fell off the carrier every corner I went round, which was only two – it was a flat ride and straight for about a mile then left into a dirt lane, then right into a road that ran along beside the river. Every time, off it slid. Throw the bike down, walk back, give the case a swift kick, pick it up put it back on the carrier. Useless.

I had forgotten most of this (see earlier sketch on memory) until recently when I was invited by a mate – actually, since a disaster of a cross-country ski trip a few years ago, not a mate I now see regularly. We knew each other from golf. He rides every week early in the morning with a bunch of similarly aged old blokes. They meet at seven o'clock at a designated spot, then mount up and ride a few kilometres, where they hop into a café for a coffee. Here they are in their monogrammed riding attire sipping coffee and eating a variety of muffins and toast. The first time I turned up, I took my road bike out of the boot of the car and attached the front wheel. How good is it that you can whip the wheels off and sling it all in the boot if you need to take it somewhere? Can't remember anyone taking my school bike anywhere. Rode it to school, to cricket, pretty much everywhere.

So I bunged the wheel on, got the helmet out while my mate – who rides an e-bike from home to the meeting place and was already set up – chatted, then over comes this other bloke and straight up asks me, 'How long have you been riding?' Funny question, I thought. Let me see, if I start from high school, perhaps almost sixty years. If I go back to primary school, even longer. But did he mean riding, or riding? Did he mean had I started riding a few minutes ago, like some of the blokes there? My mate, for example, with the e-bike. Not more than a year or so. I've ridden irregularly and owned a bike most of my life. Went everywhere by bike in the 1970s. Rode to work, rode around the place, took the bike and camping gear on the train and rode around different parts of the country. Mostly without mishap, although a half empty beer can whizzing past my head on a back road was a bit disconcerting.

The upshot of this vignette is that the ride was about twenty-five kilometres long. It was, I thought, a pleasant thing to do on a Tuesday morning. But I didn't get invited back. Well, I did, but I didn't. I made it on to the mobile text list which was sent out by a curmudgeonly bloke the night before the ride with the destination and other relevant information. I was away for the two weeks after my first effort and for some curious reason was removed from the list before I had a chance to get back in the saddle. Well, let me say I wasn't particularly perturbed. Who wants to ride a bit then sit around for an hour in lycra and padded shorts arguing about global warming? My mate said I didn't seem committed. Committed? What was this? A competition? Well, evidently it was and I treated it like a bit of fun.

I sometimes ride with my son. He covers a couple of hundred kilometres a week and is as fit as a fiddle. But when I ride with him, which is infrequently, he lolls along letting me enjoy myself. Nice. No pressure, no competition, just a pleasant ride. Which is good because at seventy, body parts no longer do what they're supposed to do. Legs that once pushed pedals for hours now fail after about thirty kilometres. I mean ten. And that's over flat ground. From the perspective of the seventy-year-old, cycling has become very competitive and very expensive. I have a nice bike but only because my son lent it to me. I would not be able to afford, nor would I see the relative value in owning, a bike that costs thousands of dollars. I would not use it enough to justify the expense. I had difficulty forking out $200 for a set of second-hand lawn bowls when I took up the game a few years ago. And a new set for $600 is still out of the question.

Bowls is an interesting game. A few years ago, those who were in charge of all things constitutional decided it needed a makeover, a new look, so they got rid of the whites and made everyone wear clown outfits. Old blokes, and there are some really old blokes who still bowl and bowl very well, looked smart and well-dressed in their whites, or creams. Now they get togged out in an array of bright-coloured shirts and matching pants or shorts that all seem to have been designed by someone who admired Roy Lichtenstein. You know, the *Whaam! Drowning*

Girl and *Look Mickey!* American pop artist and contemporary of Andy Warhol and Jackson Pollock.

Bright yellow, green, blue and purple shirts emblazoned with lightning bolts seem to be the most popular. And dispensed with cotton. Now the shirts are full polyester. If we continue the pop art motif of the 1970s, then polyester is probably a good choice but for practical purposes, in the heat of summer, not so much. In fact, downright stupid.

As we age, the choices of games we had when we were younger have been whittled away. As long as we can maintain an upright position, there are a few options still open. Bowls is one. Golf another. Too many moving parts required for cricket or tennis. And baseball, as well as hockey or soccer? Definitely out. Bowling clubs outside the major cities and large towns struggle to maintain members. Golf carts are part of the problem. Many old blokes who, if they had to walk, would have given up the putting greens and taken to the bowling greens. Now they have the option of buying a relatively cheap second-hand cart and motoring towards the precipice rather than shuffling towards it. Good for golf, not so good for bowls. Some community-spirited players try to do both – golf a couple of times and bowls once a week.

Another part of the problem appears to be a lack of motivation. By the time we hit seventy, we're less inspired to take up new activities or ventures. There are of course those mentioned above, the neo-cyclists, the avant-bushwalkers, the gymnasts whose mission for the remainder of their lives seems to be annoying everyone else with their incessant chatter about how much they spend on cycling gear and bushwalking gear and gym gear. There's a wonderful market keen to absorb their retirement income. In the old days, one wore whatever was at hand to ride or run or walk. Bushwalking required a pair of pink woollen socks, a pair of Dunlop Volleys, an oilskin coat and a woollen shirt. All other items of apparel were whatever you had to hand. A quick look at an 'outdoor' website such as Jackson's in Northern Ireland, or Cotswold's in England, gives you an idea of how much stuff you can buy and how much you can spend, and it is a shedload.

A recent trip with the almost-former-cycling-mate to what is advertised as Three Capes Walk in Tasmania demonstrated the abundance of Millennial morons who have been suckered by all the gear. This was no country for old men. We suffered an almost fatal attack of pessimism on arrival at the first of the three sleeping quarter huts on the first day out. After an underwhelming boat ride from Port Arthur to the start of the walk, the distance was not more than a couple of kilometres across which were strewn more than fifty people whose age range, if you removed us two, was all of thirty-five. And they had already taken up every conceivable bench space and spread their gear out so that it looked and smelt like a Hong Kong laundry. Worse was the fact that the bunk rooms were mixed. We were expected to bed down with young ladies who thought nothing of stripping off and standing around in their underwear. Yeah, right.

On arrival, we were greeted by a 'hut manager', a girl of no more than a score of years who proceeded to offer an 'acknowledgement of country'. Everyone except my mate stood or sat in reverent silence while it was delivered. The Australian government's National Indigenous Australian Agency provides guidelines for acknowledgement. A welcome to country can only be performed by a traditional custodian. An acknowledgement can be undertaken by anyone but mainly at significant meetings, according to the NIAA. The acknowledgement spoken at the hut on the track in Tasmania preceded outline advice on safety and cleanliness. Other examples of its use are online Zoom and Teams meetings where there are a few participants, and small community clubs making announcement about coming events. Acknowledgement of country has effectively replaced all acknowledgement of loyalty to the king. It may even be difficult to find a portrait of HRH King Charles III in any place other than RLS clubs. We shall discuss this transfer of values elsewhere.

Television

Television. What a good name. From a mixture of Latin and Greek meaning far sight. And yet for a generation of seventy-year-olds whose first glimpse of this wonderful new technology happened in the mid-1950s in Australia, its sight has been limited to how far from the screen you position your chair. Like Maccas, when it arrived it was frowned upon and yet here it is providing entertainment every night for every seventy-year-old in every home in every corner of the country. Television stations pump out matter 24/7 365 days a year. You cannot avoid it. If you leave home with the intention of finding somewhere where there is no screen presence, you'll be disappointed. Your doctor's surgery (or rooms; there's very little surgery undertaken these days); your local pub or club; the airport; the railway station; the local café. But why would you want to get away from it? It has shaped and informed your whole life. It has framed your social, cultural, ethical and moral lives from beginning to almost end.

Okay, let's look at this in a little more detail so that it has some validity as part of this manifesto. Here we were, we seventy-year-olds, glued to the new invention, the magnificence of television. We were mere sprogs in the 1950s but we absorbed, sponge-like, American family-value shows such as *Leave It To Beaver*, *The Andy Griffith Show* and *My Three Sons*.

Leave It To Beaver was the epitome of family life. Poor young Beave got in to all sorts of strife only to be told by his dear mom that he would wait to be punished when his dad came home. This mode of operation translated into most Australian homes where there were young strife-ridden lads; trans-Pacific culture adoption via the TV screen. Australian mums sometimes took matters into their own hands. No need to wait for the old man to come home to deliver the belt, it was just as easy to yell or shake the lad into submission. *Leave It To Beaver*'s objective was to apply a moral compass to boys so that they pulled up short of doing poorly conceived things, knowing they would get a belting if they did.

A little later, the dysfunctional family arrived in the form of *My Three Sons*, where the mother is not in the picture, the boys are a bit older and the dad is ably assisted in their upbringing by an old codger they call 'Bub'. For me, Bub was a mixture of all types of weirdness. I suspect that my own home life, which consisted of two parents and a younger sibling, was more attuned to Beave and his brother Wally than to the three boys and Bub. Bub seemed to do all the housework while the dad went each day to 'the plant'. Again another difficulty in trans-Pacific translation – a plant was something that grew in the ground. I was informed years later that in America a plant was a factory.

Beave's dad went off to work each day, driving into town in his Plymouth to an office where he did what we now call professional work. June and Ward Cleaver fitted well in to Australian family life. Or, if we look at it from a different perspective, the show *Leave It To Beaver* and the nuclear Cleaver family helped shape Australian family life, giving it a reason to exist because it was easy to emulate the newly invented American television family. If that was the case, then there was also a parallel between contemporary television shows and family values. This is not to say that the *Leave It To Beaver* genre was necessarily good and today's shows, *Seinfeld, Friends, Sex and the City* were bad. It merely demonstrated that what was televised was either a reflection of life imitating art or art imitating life. You are at liberty to decide whichever depending upon your point of view.

Some of us seventy-year-olds like to think that shows like *Leave It To Beaver* provided a moral focus, whereas others believe the show was simply mirroring what was going on in the world at large. Today's television is very different but relies on the same principles for its entertainment and moral values. In what we now refer to as a post-Christian western world, everything and anything is acceptable in terms of behaviour. As Beave and his brother Wally grew older during the series, there were occasional glimpses of the sexual tension that surrounded Wally and his mates. But they were only glimpses. Imagination played a vivid role in determining the outcome.

Today there is no imagination and everything is analysed to the point of exhaustion. Even the dysfunctional family situation comedies, or sitcoms, leave nothing to the imagination. *Malcolm in the Middle* is one in which the present is used as the backdrop. A lot of others rely on nostalgia for their existence and that quite often is a failing. Back in the early days of family sitcoms, *Leave It To Beaver, Father Knows Best*, and *The Adventures of Ozzie and Harriett* lived in the world of the present rather than concocting some imaginary other world. That came much later with the invention of *The Simpsons, Family Guy* and *American Dad* where it was much easier to parody family life in cartoon form.

Television is also a medium which attempts to offer immediacy and connectivity. Despite most of the content being pre-recorded, television provides us with the fantasy that we are connected with the world around us. But it is precisely that: a fantasy. Everything we watch has been sifted and picked over by focus groups so that we are given the stuff we tell the content providers we want. Or the focus groups tell them that we want.

Contemporary television is stuffed full of what have come to be known as reality shows. Reality has replaced sitcom. Reality television is no more real than *The Simpsons*. The difference is the actors and actresses (yes, there is a distinction between the sexes, Beaver) pretend to be real people rather than actors and actresses, which is precisely what they did in the sitcoms. Even sporting fixtures have become overpopulated with actors. Rugby league is filled with players who, immediately after scoring, perform some ritual action that is not part of the game. These are not spontaneous gestures. They are planned and practised much the same as reality shows. They all have workplace health and safety people wandering around to make sure the script is followed. Importantly, we know this the same as we knew Beaver Cleaver was not a real person. Or did we? Did we, as fellow nine-year-olds, think hey, Beave isn't real, he's an actor named Jerry Mathers? Nup. Not on your life. We wouldn't have known who Jerry Mathers was, let alone that he played the part of Theodore Cleaver; we probably didn't know Theodore was Beave's real name. Well, Jerry Mathers is alive and well, having been born in 1948, so he's a couple of years into his own seventies. He has his own website.

Another aspect of early sitcoms was how they dealt with problems and that some of those problems still exist today. *The Flintstones*, for example, a fine family from the early Stone Age, often had difficulty with renewable energy. Many times we watched Fred in his car being pushed down a hill to get a 'clutch start'. Or was it a battery Tesla-type model? It was relatively silent so the energy used was most likely renewable.

The issue for us, as seventy-year-olds, is that we watch a lot more television than we did when we were younger. It's our entertainment of choice and remains relatively cost-effective until a government someday decides that, like in England, we need to pay a licence fee to own and operate one. How farcical. Television and radio licences were a feature of the 1950s and 60s. Until that day comes back, we have the many and various alternative pay options that include Netflix, Binge, Amazon Prime, Disney and Stan which we can buy and watch till we have a stroke from too much sitting around being inactive.

But there is so much to choose from. How could we not be satisfied? How could we not be contented knowing we can watch a whole series of something like *Ozark* in a few nights, a series in which the script writers have chosen 'fuck' as their word of choice and the lead character, a pint-sized urchin masquerading as a girl, uses it to punctuate every sentence. A more banal and unfortunate word that has surfaced in many television dramas is one which Philip Roth's infamous novel employed in 1970. Sadly for Australian culture, *Portnoy's Complaint*, which used the c-word as a chapter heading that included the second word crazy, was banned – a government action that only made it more desirable. A bit like David Lawrence's *Lady Chatterley*. The word is now used in a variety of contexts in television dramas, sometimes to great effect, others less so. It's use as a term of derision is appalling. It does nothing more than encourage or reinforce its use by those who wish to denigrate either sex. Although, over time, I have most often heard it used by men to describe other men, or men to describe women. The focus groups did not get that one right.

Your Car

Right then. You're seventy. Are you still driving the same car you bought ten or twelve years ago? Older? Crikey. If you are, then there are a few things you will have taken note of during the preceding decade or two. Yes, your car is now considered vintage and when people look at it they do it with a sympathetic, wistful look that says poor old fella, still thinks he's sixteen.

The things that have become important to you and your car begin with getting in and out of the vehicle. Do you have to slide your left leg in first, then sit on the edge of the seat while your body makes its way in before squinching over into driving position? Do you have to hang on to the door frame for balance or do you still bend and flex as if nothing has changed since you were sixteen? I reckon most of us need a bit of the former. The alternative, of course, is that a few years ago you saw the writing somewhere on some wall and immediately scampered off to the SUV dealer. This was a good move. You pretended you were upgrading so you could take all your stuff with you (see *Seven Car Loads of What You Need*, Ginninderra Press, 2020). But in reality you were having so much difficulty getting in and out of the driver's side of the low-slung sedan that it became embarrassing. Specially when you had a handful of stuff – keys, wallet, sunglasses, mobile phone – that you had to pitch on to the passenger seat before you could even consider getting behind the wheel.

Once you were in, everything was fine. And it felt good to fire up the big engine with its V8-throated rumble. Well, all that disappeared in favour of making an upright entry, which is why you got the SUV. They come in all sizes and costs but I see a lot of blokes with grey or white hair in those Mazda 5s. The Mazda is a good option, right? I can imagine Welsh poet Dylan Thomas writing 'Rage, Rage Against the Dying of the Light' then popping out and driving to the local coffee shop in his Mazda 5. Or Frank Zappa. Or James Joyce. Your Mazda 5 is a sad choice for a seventy-year-old. As is any SUV, no matter how little or much it costs. Stick a few intertwined circles on the bonnet or a three-pointed star in a circle, makes no difference. It's still a front-wheel drive or all-wheel drive sedan with a balloon skin over it.

There are some good alternatives to the problem of getting in and out with ease other than falling for the SUV advertising. A Ford Mustang convertible, for example. I have never been much of a Ford man, preferring Holden, and if that means you stop reading from here, then so be it. I do like the Stang in the V8 format, though. Nice clean lines and plenty of grunt from the five-litre 340kw engine. Technology has changed rapidly in the past few years. A 2010 V8 Holden SS Commodore, for example, had a six-litre motor but drew only 270kw. An alternative could be the new Chevrolet Camaro. It's being shipped as a factory right-hand drive with a 6.2-litre V8 that draws 447kw. It's low slung but once you get the top off and stick it in the boot, then you can hop in and out all day without damaging any joints or ligaments. It's a bit on the pricey side so might be best to stick with the Stang.

Now that we have that problem out of the way – forget the SUV, forget the hybrid bloody electric bloody thingies until they start making them so they go further than the local shops before needing to be pumped up. What else is it that becomes important to us as seventy-year-olds when we hit the road? More people on the road? Yep. More people actually on the road. Actually walking in the road or the street rather than the footpath. And bikes. And scooters. E-bikes. e-scooters. Seems every manner of individual has the same rights as motorists.

There are some motorists who should never be allowed out but we'll come to them soon.

For now, let's examine the road traffic that is not motor vehicles. In the past few years, there are a lot more people walking than previously. It has partly to do with the numerous lockdowns caused by coronavirus. We weren't allowed more than five kilometres from home, so walking around the neighbourhood became a thing. But why on the road rather than the footpath? The rule in most states and territories in Australia is that it's illegal to walk on the road when there is an available footpath or grass verge. To walk on the road is to invite harm. If you walk on the road either towards oncoming traffic or with your back to traffic, there is a chance you will not be seen, and smack! Next thing you're injured or dead. Who would be at fault in that situation? The driver of the motor vehicle, of course. Don't blame the dumb-arse person in dark clothes with headphones ambling down the middle of the street.

Some street users seem more aware. The early-morning runners are pretty good. They mostly stick to the edge of the road. The question we need answered is not why they do it but why it makes us so angry when we see them do it. We want to race out and yell at them, or yell at them from the car window, 'Get off the fucking road, you morons', and sometimes we do, which is about as satisfying as nothing. Most times, they're unlikely to hear you and, even if they do, it does nothing except make you lose concentration on the task at hand, which is not only to drive but to avoid all the morons wandering in the road. In reality, they probably have as much right to the road but do they pay to have that right? Motor vehicle taxes in the form of stamp duty, registration, tolls and other indirect imposts are a burden on the motorist only; the cyclist pays nothing to use them. So it becomes more inflaming when governments truncate existing roads to install cycleways, quite often in places where there is no real use or need for them.

Another problem for us is concentration and distance. Statistics probably show that seventy-year-olds travel shorter distances, somewhere between their local shops, their club, and less frequently on holiday or to visit family. I have an aged aunt who is in a nursing home on the other side of the city. It's an eighty-kilometre round trip that takes an hour or more each way. I would like to visit her more frequently as she is my only remaining relative from my mother's generation but I don't always feel mentally or physically that I can get in the car, drive there, spend a couple of hours then drive back. If I take into account peak-hour traffic, forty-kph school zones that start at the ridiculous time of two thirty in the afternoon, and weather conditions, it has been a long time since I visited. If there were a direct public transport option, I would take it and it would cost me no more than $2.50 but there isn't so that's that.

Remember the days when you could drive for hours without needing to wee or sleep or rest or do any number of things that you now need? Preparation for a drive now seems to take as long as the drive itself. And the cost of fuel is prohibitive. Fuel cost was not something you thought about back then. Jump in, pedal-to-the-metal. You didn't even think about it. If you wanted to go somewhere, you went. In reality, nothing has changed. Fuel costs are not proportionally much greater then they were then, distances are still the same and in fact, roads and road conditions have improved significantly. Hard to remember that in the 1970s it took almost two hours more to drive from Sydney to Canberra or Sydney to Jindabyne. And yet if someone asked you today, on a Saturday arvo, after you'd been to the pub for a few hours, if you wanted to drive to the snow overnight, ski for the day and be back on Monday morning for work, you would have them sectioned. And yet, that's precisely what you may have done in the late 1970s, and done it every second or third weekend during the ski season. Your mind may still go at that pace but the old body simply will not tolerate such abuse.

Lastly, let's have a whinge about other drivers. Why is it that they seem incapable of obeying the road rules, or they drive in such a manner that they risk causing an accident? Or both at the same time. If you got your licence when it became available to you, then you've been driving now for more than fifty years. And you would have got it the first time you did the test. In those days, there were no provisional licences, no learner driver logbooks requiring 120 hours. You went down to the cop shop or the local motor registry, filled in the forms, the testing bloke got you to drive around the block and, hey presto, you got your licence. (I recall I did mine in a neighbour's new Vauxhall Viva, which was bright white with red seats and trim. The testing bloke sat there clicking his pen top but I was so busy concentrating on the road I didn't actually think about it till years later. A nice distraction technique but it didn't work!) You had probably done a few hours on your Ls and a few more earlier on a back road when your dad let you take the wheel. I was around eight or nine when my dad let me sit on his lap and steer for the first time. I remember it was exhilarating. The old grey Morris Minor side-valve puttering along at probably twenty miles an hour with me weaving back and forth along the single strip of paved road. When I got a bit older but was still too young to get my Ls, my mum asked the next-door neighbour if I could drive around her orchard. I have no idea why she agreed – I could have knocked down quite a few pear trees but nonetheless she did and I spend hours backing and turning and parking between the rows. For the first few goes, the dog ran around idiotically and barked and barked until I let him in, where he sat very quietly looking out the passenger window. My mother, bless her, said he was too scared to be out and too scared to get in but in was probably a marginally safer bet.

A new way of driving around the suburbs has got me bamboozled. I watch cars on my street and ninety per cent of the time they travel down the middle of the road. When a car comes the other way, they swerve in towards the gutter then out again around any parked car that might pose a threat to their trajectory. They do this both ways. Learner drivers in a vehicle with an instructor seem to be the worst culprits, so perhaps there is a new teaching method that uses weaving and dodging as a tactic. I can't quite grasp its significance. There's plenty of room on the street for two cars to hold their line and pass safely even if there are parked vehicles either side.

When you get to seventy, there are a lot of things that make driving less enjoyable than it might have been in earlier years. Again, the type of car you drive may improve your outlook on your driving experience. I imagine myself in a British racing green Jaguar with sunroof, cream leather upholstery, cruising along the Snowy Mountains Highway through some of the best sight curves ever built into a road, listening to Johann Bach's cello concertos. I would like to imagine myself in a Stang or a Vette but, really, how silly would I look? And what else is there? It has to be a rear-wheel drive, which limits my options (although Jaguar claims all-wheel drive with ninety per cent power to the rear). I am no lover of German automotive technology. Perhaps the Kia Stinger would be an option or the Toyota GR86 but they are small cars, which brings us back to the limitations of entry to the driver's seat. These small things become very big things if we are considering buying a new or second-hand vehicle. But then again, who said we were even looking? Perhaps the old Commodore or the Toyota Camry will do for another few years, at least until you get so old that the government coerces you into doing your driving test for a second time. It may not be quite as easy as it was in 1968. Sadly, there's a requirement in some states for you, when you turn seventy-five, to seek a medical opinion so you can continue to drive. Didn't see that coming, did you? Well, don't get too anxious or overexcited about it. What it means is that before your seventy-fifth birthday you will need to fill in a form and take it to your doctor, who will generally give you the nod. But it's not as benign as you may think. It's a step in controlling you and circumscribing your activities because you are now seen as someone who is incapable of looking after yourself or having an independent thought. Watch out.

Entertainment

We've discussed our main pastime, watching television, but what about the other things we do for entertainment, and what are our expectations of being entertained? Expense of entertainment is a key factor in what we do and don't do at seventy. We may be able to afford some things but not others, or we may find ourselves unable to afford any extras. Remember the days when friends or relatives would drop by on a Sunday afternoon? No invitation, no advanced planning (timeboxing they call it these days) just a visit and a bit of time spent having a cuppa or sitting around talking about stuff, having a laugh. That was prime entertainment. The impromptu nature of the visit was enough to lift your spirits, especially on Sunday arvos, which seemed to be very long and lonely.

    A typical scenario might have been you and your family going about your business doing three-tenths of sweet bugger all then lo and behold a car pulls up out the front and in come your mates from up country. They might bring a home-made cake or they might bring nothing. Didn't matter. Pop the kettle on, stick a few Orange Slices on a plate and sit around the kitchen table or the dining table or go outside and have a yarn. And they were good yarns. When you were younger, you could listen to the oldies yakking about this or that interspersed with great peals of laughter. Nothing serious on Sunday arvo over a cuppa.

Doesn't happen any more. Everything is timeboxed to within an inch of its life. Compartmentalised and workshopped so that no time is wasted. Was your Sunday arvo wasted? Never. There were plenty of gaps between call-ins. For months at a time, especially in winter, there would be nothing. Then, come spring, the pop-ins began again. Entertainment was cheap. Don't misunderstand, this isn't a call for a return to the 'great old days', because they weren't all great. It's more a reminisce that spontaneity has been lost to compartments. Perhaps we think other people's time is too important for us to waste an afternoon calling in. They may not be home, they may be busy, they may be entertaining already. When we gather at someone's place, it's always referred to as them entertaining us. I heard recently a woman comment on Covid 19 that it had robbed her of her spontaneity. But I suspect that age had already done that. Covid was a justification.

We might entertain ourselves in a variety of ways. 'What do you do for entertainment around here?' was a frequent refrain when we were younger and we could be off at the drop of a hat to listen to live music, go out for drinks and something to eat, see a film, or all of them in the same night. Now we need to plan ahead and keep our entertainment mostly to the daylight hours. If we do venture out at night, it's not likely we will make it past ten o'clock, specially if we haven't had a nana nap during the day. McDonald's knows how to present itself as entertainment. It advertises its app and free food with two old people pitching their chips into a paper plate then getting excited because their 'free' McFlurry is brought to their table. And they have two spoons! The old people are presenting as being fed and entertained at the same time in the middle of the day. Clever Maccas. If they threw in some live music, the bags of bones would be back there every day.

When we get to seventy, we have a tendency to be drawn to the attractions of seaside living. In actual fact, most coastal towns and villages are more like aged-care facilities on a larger scale. Some aged-care facilities such as RSL Lifecare at Narrabeen on Sydney's northern peninsula are set out on huge acreage with loads of entertainment such as lawn bowls, bingo, more lawn bowls and more bingo. Coastal towns are no different. Most have the added advantage of a golf course. As you age, golf is not so entertaining to you as it is to others watching you. Some coastal towns have added luxury entertainment venues. One on the north coast of New South Wales has built a bowling alley on one of its car parks. Country clubs in coastal towns have very little to offer. Bingo, darts, cards, indoor bowls, a TAB and poker machines. There the list ends. Entertainment provided by government is sporadic. Libraries and community centres create events and pretty much anything is well-attended because the townspeople are bored witless most of the time and if it rains then the outdoor stuff is doomed. Entertainment in cities – concerts, ballet, theatre – is relatively constant but prohibitively expensive, especially for those now on a pension or other fixed income. Some like to think that walking kills two birds – it's entertaining and it keeps them fit. But even the same beach walk gets boring after a while. The entertainment value quickly subsides.

Earlier generations found entertainment in strolling to the park or to the beach, where they could sit and watch others playing, or surfing, or generally having a good time. It generated their own sense of wellbeing; a visceral observation of life in full bloom. You can't do that any more. Someone will be offended that you are staring at them or that you're a kiddy diddler waiting for your chance to whisk their little Oscar or Olivia off the swings and in to the bushes. So you don't go and sit in the sun and enjoy being a part of what's going on.

There are many hurdles and barriers to stop you doing what seems natural, to funnel you in to fabricated events so that you can be kept in check, where you act and say what is expected of you as an older person, where your opinions and knowledge are smiled upon gratuitously, and where you can whittle down the days you have left without offending, irritating or outraging.

Wearing a beige cardigan helps in this. Slippers might be a bit extreme when going out but you could try adding a pair of beige trousers or even blue jeans to make yourself totally invisible. You can pick the over-seventies men because they still think wearing blue jeans is cool. They wear them everywhere, in summer with their shirts hanging out and in winter with a beige jumper or cardigan. And a flanno shirt in winter. And a Kathmandu fleecy-lined zip jacket. And there you have it. The finely dressed man ready for anything. Some go to extremes and wear black jeans. Tight ones with a bit of elastic in the legs. Works if you're skin and bone but the beer gut folding over the top of the blacks is not a good look. Better to stick with the straight-leg blue jeans. Once you've dolled yourself up, the main entertainment is the pub or the club where you used to go to crack on. Now, sadly the only thing you crack is the ring-pull on a beer can because you don't like how they pour the draught.

Clubs have what is known as a happy hour most afternoons. The hour can be expanded in some places. It is most often around three p.m. or four p.m., times when you can buy your schooner for a few cents less than regular price. Schooners are a common glass size in New South Wales: 425ml or 15oz. Other states have other names and sizes which used to provide entertainment when you visited those places because you'd ask for a schooner and the barman would tell you in no uncertain terms it was called a pot or a fifteen or some other equally stupid name. A schooner in the Northern Territory is 600ml or one pint. There are other smaller sizes such as a middy and a pony in NSW. Ponies were popular in summer in the 'old' days when the heat meant your schooner would be warm by the time you saw the bottom of the glass. A pony, at 140ml, or 7oz, stayed cold because you drank it in half the time. Other entertainment prospects around beer include discussions of what drop is best, new or old, mid-strength or light and now, for the fainthearted, the addition of zero alcohol pseudo-beer which, to my mind, defeats the purpose entirely. Those who drink it have become advocates and it's hard to stop them preaching. If they weren't so serious, they might be entertaining.

The Four-hour Rule

Right then. Let's think about this for a while. What things do we as seventy-year-olds do and for how long do we do them? As a rule, we do nothing for more than four hours. It has come to pass that once we exceed four hours, we are generally unable to continue. And why would we? Four hours is the length of time it takes to play eighteen holes; the length of time of a bowls match; the length of time we can remain asleep before we have to wee; the length of time we can tolerate talking to others; the length of time we can spend on an aeroplane; the length of time we can read a book; the length of time we can watch television. The list is endless. But not the time. Four hours seems to be the limit for most activities and events that we encounter. Remember your working life? Start at nine a.m. and break for lunch at one p.m. Four hours. A four-hour shift is standard for most volunteer organisations. After four hours, we tend to lose concentration, go off script and begin to fidget. Four hours is probably all we could manage if we were lucky enough to have any sexual encounters. More like four minutes, I hear you mutter.

So we have what we might call the Four-hour Rule. This will be a good thing for us to adhere to, especially when we're asked to childmind, babysit, chauffeur, or go shopping. There could be certain times, if we were to find ourselves in such situations, when we might want to extend the rule. We ought to be wary, though, of doing so. Much better to stick to four hours and keep out of trouble than to dive right in and spend the day, or the day and night, then find yourself in deeper than you originally intended. Lunch or dinner, perhaps a drink, then if the opportunity presents itself, a couple of hours of happiness, but no more. Four is the limit of your capabilities and capacity. You're too old to come back for seconds.

The four-hour rule, depending upon your location, does not necessarily include travel time. Nor does it preclude a bit of drinking time. Only those living in the country have the luxury of excluding the first and adding to the second. If you live in a city, it may take you an hour to get to where you want to be to spend your four hours. And the possibility of being pulled over by the police after a couple of drinks afterwards makes the prospect less pleasant. If you live in the country, however, you probably take a few minutes to get to your chosen event, so you can have the luxury of a quiet hour or so at the end.

You can also extend the four-hour rule at night by taking drugs. An osteo paracetamol will ease the ache in the bladder so you don't have to get up in the cold for at least another two hours. If you can hold off going to bed until just before midnight, then you have the possibility of a six-hour dream run. On the other hand, if you stay drug-free and crash out at ten p.m., you'll most likely last until two a.m., which allows you another four hours after that so you can make it through until six a.m., which is your normal wake-up time anyway. Most seventy-year-olds crash before ten and wake up around six, which is a good eight hours with one interruption. Can't get much better than that.

The four-hour rule must be obeyed when having sex, driving, drinking, playing sport and reading or watching television. It's a good rule to live by when you reach seventy because all the other rules have pretty much been done away with.

How funny is this? Food businesses, those places that sell edible stuff, are supposed to use guidelines which include a four-hour rule. Studies show that food can be safely held 'out of temperature control' for short periods of time without significantly increasing the risk of food poisoning. The time that food can be safely held between 5° and 60° is referred to as the '4-hour/2-hour rule'. After four hours out of the 'zone', it has to be chucked. Fits nicely with the assisted dying rules. Be very careful how you play it and don't get out of the zone. Hilarious.

In a book on French bourgeois culture, the author says he had three talks with a Ms George H senior, a seventy-year-old retired company executive, for the purposes of writing about his life. Why four-hour sessions, we may ask? Why not six two-hour chats? Another book claims four hours is all it takes to become a professional chef (tell that to the tradie schools). The blurb for the book, entitled *The 4-hour Chef*, claims it is not 'just' a cookbook, but a 'choose your own adventure guide to the world of rapid learning'. So there's another thing you as a seventy-year-old can do in four hours: rapid learn. Get those brain-fogged coronavirus heads around that piece of useless information. What if you need to take medication? Paracetamol is, the experts tells us, a safe medication for pain relief and fever reduction. The recommended dose? One every four hours. How many doses in a day? Not more than four. What a great number. Four every four hours. But not more than four in twenty-four.

Here's the bit to top it all off. If you stick to the four-hour rule, then you probably ought to take notice of what the experts say about drinking. You guessed it. No more than four standard drinks a day. They go on to say don't have more than ten a week but simple arithmetic indicates that four a day multiplied by the days of the week does not add up to ten. Well, not in the real world. Possibly they mean if you have four today and four tomorrow then the next day you can have two then slide to zero for the next four days. There's our favourite number again. Four days booze free. Yoiks.

There's another book that has done very well for its author since it was published in 1997. It's entitled *The Four Agreements: a practical guide to personal freedom*, in which inspiration is taken from ancient spiritual beliefs that help readers transform their lives into new experiences of freedom, happiness and love. It advocates four basic agreements: be impeccable with your word; don't take anything personally; don't make assumptions; and always do your best. It got a boost from a television personality in the United States.

So here we have 'four' being important on a whole lot of levels. On your next encounter with anything, get out the stopwatch and see if you finish smack bang on four hours, If not, then you're not doing it right. Use more duct tape, as they say.

Volunteering

When they conclude their working lives, a lot of men cast around for a meaningful replacement. Often times, this is impossible and all it does is create feelings of inadequacy, redundancy and anxiety. Some retire well before they should. Some are forced out of the occupation that defines them. I remember some years ago a well-qualified solicitor with a prestigious Sydney law firm saying he was going to retire. He was fifty-five. The reason he gave was that he wanted to spend more time on his favourite pursuit of competitive sailing but the real reason, as he disclosed to me over a bottle of red and a rare Angus rump steak, was that he felt pressured. He was a banking and finance specialist and he said his experience counted for naught when he sat opposite a thirty-five-year-old bank manager who had zero interest in what a fifty-five-year-old thought or knew. So off he went taking all that accumulated experience and sailed into the sunset, or around the world or somewhere exotic. I don't actually know what he did because ours had been a business friendship and once that was severed, we lost touch. I calculate that he'd be well into his eighties if he's still above ground.

We've considered the problem of not knowing or hearing what happens to others. They say it's easy to find anybody or anything these days. All you have to do is say 'Hey, Google' into your device and everything surfaces. Well, that's not quite right. All that's available is what Google or any other search engine wants you to see.

But back to volunteering. Here you are, first day without getting up and putting on your work clothes and going off somewhere to do what you have always done. Great. Plenty of time to mow the lawn, or if you live in an apartment go for a walk and get a coffee, read the news, probably online, then make a list of all the things that need doing. A week later, they're all done. I have another mate who's planning to retire to the Gold Coast of Queensland in a few years' time. He has a few concerns about leaving children and grandchildren but makes up for it by saying he can play golf in the morning, have a couple of beers, go home and have a nap, then stroll down to the surf club for a few more quiet ones before tea. No talk of volunteering for anything, although after a few weeks of golf he may decide to do something.

Now comes the tricky part. You think it might be satisfying to volunteer for something. No idea really what but it makes you feel all warm and fuzzy that you could give your time to something for free.

Well, here are some facts and figures – not too many because they clutter up the thinking – there are already six million Australians who volunteer through some type of organisation, which is how such statistics can be measured. There are probably millions more who do voluntary work such as minding kids or shopping for neighbours but they remain uncounted. Volunteers contribute almost 600 million hours a year. And men volunteer almost as much as women, roughly 30% to 28%, which is not much different. Now here's the good one. Thirty-six per cent of volunteers come from the forty to fifty-four age group but those over seventy contributed nearly 25%.

According to Volunteering Australia, men are more likely to volunteer for sport or physical recreation (47%) while women are more likely to take on health and welfare as well as children (30%). Sixty-five per cent of men say they do it for personal satisfaction and to do something worthwhile, 32% said they did it for social contact, while 31% wanted to remain active. There are more than 56,000 not-for-profit organisations in Australia that rely on the generosity of volunteers. The latest figure from the Australian Bureau of Statistics on the monetary value of unpaid labour is from 2007, which is $14.6 billion. That's a fair whack. Of even more interest to us as we contemplate joining this vast sea of volunteers is that they feel much better about themselves than non-volunteers. Eighty-two per cent to 75% to be precise. And volunteers are more likely to provide assistance to a stranger than non-volunteers (64% to 41%). So next time you're feeling all of your seventy years and have an episode while standing in line ordering your Maccas lunch, hope that a young person with first aid experience or RFS or SES quals comes to your aid.

If you really want to spend some of your time doing things for others, you can find plenty of organisations who want you. Think of a name and look up their website. Don't be put off if there's a bit of training involved. It could be a good thing. And don't try to impose your working life regime onto the organisations you're about to join. You're a volunteer. Don't take it seriously. This doesn't mean that you should muck around. Most volunteer training is accredited and requires four elements to be recognised (there's that fab 'four' again). There are four endorsed components – units of competency; assessment requirements; qualifications; and credit arrangements. And there are four dimensions of a competent model: attitudes; knowledge; skills; and behaviour. All this training comes under the umbrella of the Australian Skills Quality Authority, a highly competent organisation that provides accreditation to courses run by registered training organisations. So give it a thrash.

Men's Organisations

There are men's organisations and then there are organisations of men. Some of the fabricated places where men gather are just that: fabrications imagined as part of a structured existence to keep us amused until we fall off the twig. Then there are others in which we can be so absorbed by the reality of them that we come away with a deep satisfaction of continuity and achievement. Men gather in groups for all sorts of reasons. Young men for sport, old men for company. Men's organisation are under attack by woke lefties and feminists (also woke lefties) simply because they are men's organisations. They exist for the benefit of men, which, in today's world, is a no-go zone. We must, according to pop culture aficionados, be inclusive and respectful. Inclusivity means allowing anyone and everyone into every organisation, which is causing some problems in schools and other places in which transgender men wish to use women's facilities and play in women-only sporting competitions.

The issue of inclusivity is complex and fraught. Organisations which have in the past been exclusively men's, such as golf and bowls competitions in which men and women played separate events, are now free to allow women to play. The men's competitions, that is. Women's competitions remain for women only. It's uncertain where the present argument about segregation will end. What is certain is that some organisations will remain men-only because women have no interest in joining. Much like women's organisations most of which men have no interest in. The Country Women's Association is one which ought to remain as its name suggests. It has a history which is respected by all. There is an argument that says women need to create their own organisations or to colonise existing institutions because men have historically dominated all areas of society, which includes creating organisations with a traditional masculine focus. If we look hard enough, these might include the houses of parliament, religion, governments and business. Masculinity has been the driving force in the creation of economies. Economies have sustained societies. Western societies are under attack for being too masculine.

Many men's organisations exist to deal with or assist men and their mental well-being. Men's Shed is probably the most commonly known, while the telephone counselling service Mensline is gaining traction. A lot of the older men's organisations, begun and sustained after the world wars, have grown into old age with their constituent members and they now have difficulty remaining relevant. Where these organisations existed for their mateship, newer organisations are established to assist men with mental illness which, by its nature, implies victimhood. Men's Shed is a good idea but there is an overtone of sadness: men have to gather in a shed, as men of older generations spent time in their own sheds. The older men spent time in their sheds then went off to volunteer with Legacy, or Lions, went off to bowls or golf, went off to the RSL or Lodge, or both at different times. In other words, they had a surfeit of mates in different places with whom they could talk and drink and generally feel good about themselves and the world in which they lived. New generations, our own 'boomer' included, lost touch with so many of those older organisations simply because we did not see a relevant attachment.

Most of us did not experience the horrors of war; we were uninterested in Freemasonry and we were too caught up in our own need for well-being to volunteer to join organisations that were there to assist others. We gave up the pleasantness of organisational mateship where there was a lot of drinking and camaraderie because laws were put in place to stop us. Random breath testing springs odiously to mind. Now we can't have more than two beers, wherever we are, for fear of being over the limit and accumulating too many demerits on our driver's licences. So off we go, when the game is over, to have a few at home. Not with mates. Which is why, partly, there is a need for organisations focused on men's mental well-being.

There are plenty of organisations for men. The difficulty lies in finding the right fit. Sports clubs – rugby clubs, golf clubs, cricket clubs – work on the basis of a mutual interest that requires at least a minimum level of fitness, both physical and mental. If you want to play, that is. I know of a good bloke who has been a volunteer, with his missus, for more than twenty-five years at a district rugby club where he coordinates and organises ball boys. Simple task, right? Think again. Barry has been coordinating ball boys for super rugby and Sydney test matches, alongside his weekly commitment to his local club, which honoured him with life membership. At the 2003 Rugby World Cup, Barry organised ball boys for all the Sydney football stadium matches.

Men's Sheds are for old blokes. Bowls clubs are for old blokes, although plenty of young blokes play at elite levels. Probus clubs are for really old blokes who also seem to frequent Men's Sheds and bowling clubs. If you haven't already learned how to, it's probably too late for the intricacies of chess, so you can't join a chess club, or a bridge club.

Do not get bogged down in the belief that there is no room for you. While it may be unfashionable to stand at your gate, or find a seat in the sun at the local park, these are places you can be with impunity. Don't stop acknowledging the young woman walking past with her toddler in a pram because you think she'll think you're a dirty old perv. She won't. Smile. You never know, it may be the restart you need.

Religion

If I had been writing this book a generation or two ago, religion, or more specifically Christianity, would have had a prominent place in the thoughts and deeds of men. Men who lived in a nominally Christian country strove to lead a Christian life; they were members of a congregation, wore coats and ties to church and sat down to Sunday lunch with their families. At least, that was the image projected. Churches were indeed full, from both sides of the Christian divide, the Catholic and the Protestant. Australia itself was still considered a Protestant nation given the slightly greater numbers of those who identified as such in national surveys. There were divisions in workplaces between 'Tykes' and 'Prods', with a predominance of Tykes in blue-collar jobs while Prods held the high ground in the white-collar work of accountants, lawyers and bankers. These lines were similarly drawn in political parties, with Labor the party of choice of the Catholic worker while the Liberal Party of Bob Menzies became the party of the conservative office worker. Men generally, and I use the word generally very loosely here, voted for the same party from early age through to older age. There were invisible lines dominated by religious beliefs which kept men anchored.

All that changed rather abruptly in the 1960s. The decade of the 60s is blamed for a lot of things but mostly the perceived freedoms that surfaced with sex and drugs and rock and roll. Many made a conscious choice to abandon everything that smelled old, following the predictions and pronouncements of the rock gods rather than the one true God of Christianity. Strength and the courage of their convictions was drawn from alternative religions such as Buddhism, while many simply abandoned any faith that did not promote the embrace of weed.

The abandonment of faith was not always related to the embrace of an alternative. My own grandfather, a good Methodist, was unable to find solace in his faith before he took his life at the age of thirty-nine, well before any hippy surfaced. For him, the horrors of World War I were too great. His service on a hospital ship in the Mediterranean and Atlantic, on which he saw so many dead and wounded, altered his very nature. On return, he married and founded a textile manufacturing business which did well enough for him to buy a house and begin raising a family, a girl and a boy. But the experience of the war remained, so that when the economic depression arrived, his business collapsed and he was forced to move with his wife and children back to the home of his mother.

It is impossible to know what he experienced and the mental toll it took on him. What can be surmised is that he found no comfort in Methodism and found no one within the church or outside it to reveal the extent of his mental illness. We call it mental 'health' now but in those days, 1939, mental health meant being mental. And being mental was reason enough to have someone sectioned. There were laws that allowed such things and additional laws that criminalised taking one's own life.

My grandfather, an intelligent man, would have known what the consequences of his actions would be. Had he been able to communicate his deep depression and anxiety, he might have been able to find a path other than the one he took. Had his father still been alive, he might have been able to help his son. His father, my great-grandfather, mentioned in the introduction, was a lay preacher in the Methodist church. His own father had converted to Methodism on arrival in Australia in 1830, having heard John Wesley preach his doctrine at Gwennap Pit in Cornwall. My great-grandfather had felt so strongly about his religion that he had, in 1912, sent to the newly created Mitchell Library in Sydney two of his father's Methodist church quarterly membership tickets. The tickets, and his covering letter, remain in the Mitchell Library, a record of his father's devotion to the church.

In those days of Methodism, a quarterly ticket was issued sparingly: if a man attended worship at least once a week and also attended a weekly prayer meeting. The Methodist church played a very important, indeed critical, daily role in the lives of its congregants. If we fast-forward to today, there is no Methodist church. It ceased to exist when other Protestant denominations, Presbyterian, Uniting and Baptist, decided to join 'forces'. The joining of the denominations killed off Methodism and mostly heralded an end to the Presbyterian church in Australia. John and Charles Wesley's great vision had come to an end, as had the Scottish church. It's ironic given that John Wesley had difficulty making inroads into Scotland during his wide-ranging travels that spread the popularity of Methodism.

Churches today, even the Catholic church, have made so many concessions to populist culture that it is difficult to determine precisely where the core of Christianity lies. And if it's difficult to grasp what Christianity is all about, then it becomes difficult to reconcile one's continuing faith. Which is probably why so many men, either approaching seventy or somewhere past it, refrain from attending services on Sundays. There are too many alternatives. If you're out and about on a Sunday, how many people to do you see sitting on some footpath outside a café worshipping their mug of coffee? Sitting on boxes or milk crates discussing climate change? Or striding or running along the road in 'active wear' actually in the road so that motor vehicles must make way for them. If a motorist were to hit a jogger, who is inevitably jogging with the traffic and unconcerned about their safety, it would be the motorist who would be liable, even though the law states it is illegal to walk on the road when there is a footpath or grass verge available, as discussed above.

But back to worship. Many churches which had traditional eleven a.m. services found that they were losing worshippers because there is no longer the Sunday family lunch but a mixture of 'brunches', a strange American term that means combining breakfast and lunch. Brunch is a way to get around the fact that you slept in but are still keen enough to go out without wasting the whole afternoon on lunch.

Church congregations today are comprised mostly of older women. Many are widowed but those with husbands find the husbands are less interested in the service because it no longer has a real focus. Too many exogenous variables have come in to play so that the core message of Jesus gets lost in the ruins.

Some time ago, I attended service in St John's Parramatta, New South Wales, the church where my great-great-great-great-grandparents were married by Reverend Samuel Marsden in 1805. I'm not a regular worshipper at this church but I had been a couple of times, though I would not expect the priest to remember me nor would I expect him to come and sit next to me and introduce himself giving only his Christian name. But this he did. It was a bit disconcerting. I want the priest or minister to remain at arm's length from me. I want him to receive the word of God and to pass it on to me. I want to be able to call him Reverend such and such, not Steve or Dave or Mike. I want to be able to show respect for the man of God and for him to act with reverence as is his calling. On this occasion, things got even sillier. When we were leaving, we stopped to admire the architecture of the outside of the building, a design that had come directly from Elizabeth, the wife of the great governor, Lachlan Macquarie. While we were standing there, a very nice woman of Chinese heritage, because that's how we must refer to them, rushed over and asked, 'Would you like me to take photo of you?' We politely declined but she insisted, because 'this church very old, very nice to have photo'.

On another occasion, I attended a service in the church where I was married more than forty years ago. I had not returned in the intervening years because we moved to another part of the city. It was what could only be described as an Anglican service that was attempting to virtue signal itself to everyone other than men. It was impossible to grasp what the young male priest was trying to say and what lesson he was striving to reveal. But it was anything but inclusive, because he made numerous apologies on behalf of men who he believed had perpetrated an infinite number of crimes and sins. It was an unpleasant service. It did inspire me, though. It inspired me to check it against online services that became popular during the coronavirus pandemic. And what I found disappointed me. These services are also attempting to be all things to all people. Except men.

Politics

As you get older, you're supposed to swing away from radical politics and move more into the conservative or centre-right of the sphere. What I've discovered since turning seventy is that many seventy-year-old men I meet have yet to lose their 'progressive feel good' ideologies. They remain, as Laura Nader said of the academies, radical in the abstract but intolerant of direct political action. What this means is that they're still angry about governments that don't do what they expect them to do while at the same time they have their annual overseas holiday, drive their European SUVs and belong to private golf clubs. For most of us, this is simply pie in the sky – we need to watch our fixed income as the cost of living expenses increase dramatically even to the point where a couple of cold beers now costs upwards of $14. And the price of fuel when it gets over $2.50 a litre is beyond comprehension to most of us. Yet so many of the progressives who hated Donald Trump with an ideological passion do nothing to contribute by way of direct political action because they might get their hands grubby.

Then there are those in their seventies who wander about calling themselves anarchists. It's relatively easy to do that in most democratic countries. No one cares and no one is likely to challenge you. You can say anarchist when you mean progressive because generations of youthful activists from the MeToo culture don't actually know what an anarchist is or does. Sounds good but.

When you get to seventy, you no longer trust government. Not because you don't need to but because you cannot. You have enough experience to know that whatever they're doing, they're not doing it on your behalf. Government is different to politics. You don't expect to trust a politician, just like you can never trust a journalist to write or speak truthfully. There's always an angle. Politicians are the same. The problem is that government is supposed to be trustworthy. Again, not politicians but the government that runs your country ought to be able to be trusted to know what they're doing and to know what to do next no matter what the circumstances, risk or future.

The planning and 'strategising' ought to be based upon what has happened in the past and what that will mean for the future. You must be able to trust that your library will open when it says it will; your grocery store will stock enough milk and bread and eggs for when you need to buy them; your pharmacist will have the right ingredients to make up the medications you need when you need them, or when your medical practitioner prescribes them. We used to call our medical practitioners doctors. And we used to be able to see the doctor when we were sick. Or he, and they were generally male, would come to you. He knew your history and he usually knew what to do for you when you took ill.

Governments deregulated medical practitioners. Corporate medicine provides us with doctors who outsource everything. If you can find one to examine you in the first place. You might turn up at a medical practice one week and see someone, then next time it's someone else who looks at a screen to check your health record. And that works if the previous person you saw has uploaded everything. If not, then it's a quizzical look and the inevitable question 'What seems to be the matter?' The matter of course is what you came to see the medico about, trusting that they would look at you and diagnose. It can happen that you sometimes get a good one. I presented at a country hospital a few years ago with a dreadful pain in my stomach right at the belt line. The nurse on duty took one look at me and said, 'Renal colic, come in here straight away', which I gladly did, much to the chagrin of the ten or so patients in the waiting room.

On occasion, there will be a politician with similar capabilities. They take one look at society and know what it needs to get better. It doesn't have to start out being sick but every society, at least western democratic societies, look to improve the lot of their citizens. That is why they exist. And as we enter our seventh decade, we find it easier to spot the fakes from the real. Years of practice will do that. I can't name one from a government in any democracy who presents as real and does real things. At least not one with centrist or right of centre sympathies.

The current popularity of anti-colonialism drives most centrists underground or to the sidelines where they think they are less likely to come under attack. One cannot speak today in positive terms of early British, American, Australian or European history without encountering what is curiously named 'cancel culture'. There appears to be a diffuse movement intent upon eradicating everything and anything to do with what the movement self-describes as the practice and policy of control by one group of people or power over other people. Such a broad description allows everything to be bulldozed because everything done in the name of democracy can be defined as power of one over another.

This is partly why politicians are terrified of saying or doing anything that is not bound up in the triple virtues of achieving net zero carbon dioxide emissions; expunging toxic masculinity; and eliminating sex stereotypes. Politicians on the left believe there is only one game in town and that is that the world is divided into the oppressed and the oppressors. The emergence and occupation of governments – local, provincial and national – by those who believe in the ideology of Marxism and the virtue of critical race theory has taken place during the past fifty years. The love and peace of the 1960s, which we as seventy-year-olds played very little part in because we were mostly still in school, transformed into a hard left ideology of hatred for everything conservative or traditional. So much so that conservative values have been trashed beyond recognition.

Political parties now look to opinion polls before making pragmatic choices. There is little to distinguish between major parties in two-party preferred systems as in Britain, Australia, the USA, Canada and New Zealand. Whoever is in control of the treasury benches in a democratic country is now busy demonstrating the art of appeasement or kowtowing.

Kowtow is an interesting word, one which has its origin in China. An emperor is said to have expected anyone presenting themselves to 'kowtow'; to kneel and touch the ground with the forehead in a demonstration of excessive subservience. A famous example is the Macartney mission led by George Macartney in 1792 to meet Chinese emperor Qianlong. The mission was sponsored by the East India Company and blessed by King George III. Macartney's was the first diplomatic mission to China but it failed spectacularly because Macartney refused to kowtow to Qianlong.

More than 200 years later, politicians and diplomats have reversed Macartney's position and now kowtow to all and sundry who shout loudly about global warming, misogyny and colonialism. The problem for the generation of politicians and civil servants now in power is that most were born during the past forty years, a period of extended peace and economic growth. Who remembers eighteen per cent interest rates on housing loans? Not them. Who remembers transport and dock worker strikes? Not them. It's easy to run a policy of appeasement when you know very little about what or whom you are attempting to appease.

Not all elected representatives are fooled into believing the climate extremists and man haters, though. Many of them share the ideologies and to avoid scrutiny clothe their rhetoric in questionable positions. The 'what if we don't do anything' scenario is a good one. The bandwagon is pretty full of these characters evangelising across the world. At least across the western world where 'white' men are now seen as the creators of everything evil. Coal is enemy number one. Coal for burning in power stations, that is. Coal for steel-making seems to have missed out on the opprobrium for the time being. Thermal coal is the monster.

It is burned to create energy which is converted to electricity which in turn is converted into heat and light. Complex processes delivering simple effects. Heat your food, light your house, power your computer and television, warm or cool your house as desired. It's often referred to as baseload power, which means it's there at peak times such as morning and evening when people need it most. Baseload remains static and coal-fired power stations are probably the cheapest form of baseload power.

Nuclear is pretty good too but western democracies which have employed nuclear power without too much adverse reaction are being driven to shut them down much the same as coal-fired stations are being taken offline to reduce carbon monoxide. It is, according to Marxist ideology, carbon monoxide emitted by coal-fired power stations – fossil fuels – that causes much global warming. And there is evidence of the contribution of anthropogenic climate change to global warming. Nuclear power, however, emits no carbon monoxide. Simply put, electricity from nuclear power is created by boiling water to make steam that drives turbines. It is an attractive alternative to coal as a baseload energy source. About the only spot in the world where there is no nuclear power is Australia, due to a government policy of anti-uranium mining dating from the 1980s.

As you get older, you get more time to think about things. In younger age, as already mentioned, much gets in the way and we take a lot of things for granted. Local government is a good example. No one takes much notice, especially anyone who does not own property. After all, local government 'rates' are really taxes by another name imposed on property owners who get very little bang for their buck. Everyone gets to vote for local councils but who in their right mind would nominate for election to an organisation that does nothing more than collect rubbish, and, if the mood takes them, fix roads?

As good citizens, we pay our rates, or taxes, which are based on the market value of our property. When the value goes up, so too our taxes, but have you noticed that when values are static, or drop, even marginally, there is no drop in taxes? They rise every year. We rarely question the taxes imposed for collecting rubbish and fixing roads. My own local government impost is around $2,500 a year. For that, I get three garbage bins into which I must subdivide items so they look virtuous. No grass clippings in the red bin, no cardboard in the green bin, no food scraps in the yellow bin, for example. While I might pay what seems an excessive amount, no one comes to help me pack the bins or drag them to the kerb for collection. In fact, my local government asks me to pay for the privilege of doing so. I suppose this is why they call themselves councils. As if they're sitting at a round table like the Hobbit coalition in *Lord of the Rings*, ready to fight evil and thinking of the best things they can do for us.

We get far too much governing, so 'council' must seem like a soft alternative. Same with rates. But what if our 'council' goes slanting off and starts involving itself in things that don't concern it – matters that lie outside its purview, which is pretty much everything except roads and rubbish. My council distributes a little glossy brochure extolling its virtues. The front indicates it's the summer/autumn issue but I have never seen one before so have no idea if this is a one-off. It has nice smiley mugshots of the fifteen councillors on the outside back cover; seven men and seven women which may justify the inside front cover message from the lady mayor that she looks forward to leading this inclusive and diverse council so that the city grows and flourishes. She also writes that she looks forward to serving her community and helping the city through 'challenging times'. There's no further detail on what the challenging times might be – perhaps the nonsense statement that the council is at once inclusive and diverse. Indeed a challenge.

But I digress. Neither the lady mayor nor I suspect my own local 'ward' elected representatives are planning to come around and help me sort my garbage. So what am I paying for? When I go out the front on the morning of delivery, which I often do to see which bins will be collected first, I note that the collection trucks are not labelled with a local government name. Rather they're a private contractor. A quick look at the contractor's website provides a few numbers – many millions provided with waste collection services; millions provided with clean drinking water and other millions with waste water treatment. So they know their stuff. Or do they?

Further on, it states that they take the time to understand their customers, that they're always one step ahead and that they partner with communities to empower sustainable living practices and support organisations working to protect the planet. Makes sense in a way. If they didn't collect the garbage, it would build up and build up and life would get pretty unsustainable – piles of garbage rotting away in the summer sun and rain. Good idea to understand their customers. Thought that might be a given. Reminds me of the advertising bloke in the series *Mad Men* sitting around contemplating, 'What do women want?'

But back to the garbage. The contractor's second of four core values is their embrace of diversity. Well, that too makes sense – different bins for different rubbish. The council, as we note above, provides inclusivity, which must mean they will collect all the bins inclusively without disrespecting the different colours.

Let's look at this seriously for a moment. Here we have an organisation taking taxes from approximately 85,000 private residential dwellings. Not all of them pay the same amount. An average might be $1,500. Revenue from taxes would then be around $127 million. Council doesn't provide details of its income. It offers an overview of operational and capital expenditure with operational for 2021 being $266 million.

Let's give council a bit of a hand. I propose contacting the garbage contractor directly and negotiating a fee for service. I will then have a clear idea of how much it costs to collect my garbage. I will also save a bit because I won't need to pay for my council to invest in matters that don't concern it. There are 600,000 charities in Australia and 257,000 NGOs (non-government organisations) which are there to keep us safe from global warming, nuclear energy, toxic masculinity and ourselves. Local government is government, not non-government or charitable therefore it does not need to become involved where it has no expertise or capability. There are more than ten million NGOs, yes 10,000,000. That's a lot of organisations around the world that are neither governments nor corporations.

Perhaps American writer Henry David Thoreau is partly responsible for the demise of big government. Remember when you were not seventy, when you were younger and most things were owned and run by the state? The railways, the roads, the power stations, all owned and operated by the state. At the time, we thought they were inefficient but hey, have another look now at privatised power costs and how much you pay to drive on private toll roads. Also look at how little freight is carried on rail. Thoreau was a child of the nineteenth century, yet his thoughts and opinions took a stronger hold in the twentieth. In his time, he was imagined to be an impractical reformer but his thesis, that government is best which governs least, and further, that government is best that governs not at all, went to the heart of late twentieth century privatisation.

There were many experts then telling us, persuading us, that private was better because governments could then get on and do things for us more directly, such as building better hospitals and providing better living conditions. Governments have been infiltrated by those who take no interest in the practicalities of providing better living conditions. Their horizon stretches only as far as the end of the inner city street in which they live. Anyway, who needs new hospitals or wider provision of aged-care services? Old peeps ought to go off and die rather than taking up valuable resources that could be better invested in coffee shops, wind turbines and solar panels. The turbines and panels can be sent off to the countryside where no one lives, but more coffee shops in the inner city please. Future aged-care services become academic as legislation in most Australian states now allows governments to kill the old and the infirm. Governments argue that the old and infirm can choose to live or die but future governments may see there is no choice and it will be bye bye boomers.

Commodities

By commodities, we mean the things we buy and consume. The things we buy in the expectation that they will last a long time. If not a lifetime. Some things have a guarantee of a lifetime. I suspect that doesn't mean seventy years. There's probably a product statement attached that has in small print that a lifetime guarantee means it might last for ten or twenty years. As seventy-year-olds, we have very different expectations of product life cycles to thirty-year-olds. This has partly to do with fashion. We may buy furniture because it's solid and long-lasting rather than fashionable and ready to be ditched in three or four years' time. What's important is to distinguish or differentiate between form and function. I have a small bar refrigerator that belonged to my dad. It's not real big but it sits in the garage and when necessary ices around fifteen or sixteen cans and a couple of bottles of white. It's one of those old rounded-corner jobs that's made to look like it's wood-panelled. It functions perfectly well but in terms of form, well, it wouldn't make it into a retro art installation and I would have to pay someone to take it away. But it does the trick.

From my observations and conversation with those of the generation we have produced, and the one below them, our sense of history is very, very different. I have difficulty coming to terms with a lot of the things they say and do. Commodities and their form and function are only part of it. Actions today or the actions taken by Millennials seem to require an enormous amount of detail and explanation of the action before and after it's taken. When they contemplate taking an action, or acting in some way, they require a plan to be put in place that provides not simply an outline but a fine detail of what will transpire with the act. Spontaneity is a thing of the past. Every act is contemplated, investigated, discussed and either accepted or rejected before it is acted upon.

While they ditch everything that happened before 2000, including being uninterested in their own family histories, they're at pains to construct a history of themselves that seems to involve a need to have an awareness of every detail and to choreograph every act so that it fits a narrative that they believe is correct or will be correct historically when it comes time to examine it. Their history will be one of the most boring, mundane list of acts and episodes in the history of the world. But it won't matter because it will be the only one. Their memory of everything else doesn't exist because they're unwilling to imagine that there could have been history before them. The epoch will probably be referred to as HOMO – History of Millennial Observations. Their actions will be inconsequential because they were boiled in detail beyond recognition.

Yet they for some inexplicable reason adhere themselves to various events in history that have become obsolete; events or celebrations that were based on actions that took place so long ago that their meaning, now the original inhabitants are dead, ought to be consigned to the past – to become memories rather than continuing celebrations.

One such is the Australian and New Zealand commemoration of Anzac Day on 25 April. I will gain no friends or admirers for writing this but I suspect Anzac Day ought to have been buried with the last of the World War II diggers it inspired. As a child and youth, I was involved in Anzac Day celebrations. My father served as a gunner in the 2/7th Field Regiment in World War II and my paternal grandfather as a sergeant in the Army Medical Corps in World War I. I was taken to dawn services, I donned my Scout uniform and marched down the high street of our town while my father marched with his compatriots. I recall clearly (here's that memory disk again whirring around) him leaving early on Anzac morning to catch a train into the city to march with members of his battalion. Of all the things in his wardrobe that I admired, his service medals stand out. My house was burgled a few years back and the medals were stolen. I have no idea why anyone would steal such things but it didn't make me angry or upset. I suppose I was sad but their loss served as a tipping point for me. Perhaps it was time to leave the commemoration of that event in Turkey and to move on. In younger years, for me, it was the excitement of getting dressed up and marching with a lot of bands making noise. I didn't see any of the after events, the drinking, the gambling that went with it and which today are the only remaining things being celebrated.

Millennials make a big thing out of going to Anzac Cove in Turkey and standing around at dawn wrapped up against the coolness of the middle-eastern spring air. Television cameras capture their sad faces as they contemplate an event that happened more than a hundred years ago, a destructive event that had horrific ramifications in Australia for many years. It's an event that no longer has currency, as all who participated are dead. The Sydney march, much like other marches in other capital cities, is now comprised of emergency service people and a few regulars in the defence forces along with some remnants of the Vietnam War, and Australia's involvement in Timor, Iraq and Afghanistan. But those wars were very different. The route no longer traverses its historic path along George Street. The television cameras, the personalities who once had an intimate knowledge of every regiment as they rolled past the cameras, have ceased, just as the guns of World War I ceased so long ago.

If they don't need history to guide them in other aspects of their lives, they also don't need to reshape the tragedies of World War I and World War II to become place markers for something they cannot possibly apprehend. Just as I, with my limited understanding of my father's and grandfather's involvement, see no real need for it to continue as an event that shapes our future.

Income & Investments

I know of seventy-year-olds who have accumulated wealth and I know others who scrape by on a government pension. While I'm not terribly numerate myself, I do know that income must exceed outgo if you're to continue to feed, clothe and house yourself. Income is a funny word that really means money coming in. It's often subdivided into other words that make it more important, such as wages and salary, commissions, grants, pensions or subsidies.

The federal government provided what it called a 'cost of living bonus', which was $250. That is income. It comes in to your bank account and, until you spend it, it will remain there. It does not accumulate interest, which is what banks used to give you for depositing your money with them. Think about it for a moment. You give the bank your money to do what they like with, and they promise to give you a little bit of additional money which they call interest. So it's in your 'interest' to give them money to look after it for you so that you'll get a little extra from them for the privilege of using your money to make a profit for themselves. Banks make large profits but they no longer give you interest on the money you give them to make their profits. The reason they no longer give you interest is that they appear to no longer need your money to keep them liquid.

Liquidity, as I understand it, is when a bank has enough money on hand to pay out every person who comes and asks for their money back if and when they need it. So why do we give our money to banks if they give us nothing in return? Indeed, they offer us a variety of credit in the form of plastic cards that are the equivalent of the money we deposit with them. They use quaint words like 'deposit' but in effect there is no alternative for us unless we do what former Australian Prime Minister Malcolm Fraser advised and keep our savings under our mattresses. Even today, this is out of the question because every piece of income, from our pension to our superannuation to our share holdings, if we have any, are 'deposited' directly for us into our bank accounts. The banks charge us fees for these 'transactions' and if we don't pay off our credit cards each month, they charge us additional fees. On top of that, they charge us an annual fee to have the luxury of using the card. Technology has advanced a lot in recent years, so even the credit card is becoming obsolete for new generations of consumers. It's easy now to have your bank details inserted in your smartphone so that when you buy something, all you have to do is tap your phone on a little machine at the point of sale and, presto, you've paid. Electronic funds transfer at point of sale is what this is known as, or the initialism eftpos. It is not, as some argue, an acronym. There are very few true acronyms, one being scuba and others being laser and radar.

Let's look at some of the forms of income and investments available to us as seventy-year-olds. Whatever they may be, we can be certain that there are comparative limitations to how we come by them. Very few of us at seventy remain in what is known as the workforce. Work and force are interesting words to use in combination. Now that we're out of it, we can appreciate far more that it was indeed forty or forty-five years forced out of us because we had to feed, clothe and house ourselves and our families.

I recall that my father obtained a war service home loan after he married. It was a fixed interest loan set at around two per cent. My mother gave him a hard time about it for years, arguing that they ought to have paid it off, everyone else had and they didn't own their house et cetera. What she seems to have failed to apprehend was that while they were paying off the loan at two per cent, any accumulated funds in the bank from my father's public service wage were earning interest at roughly the same rate, so the loan was costing them nothing.

In 2010, when we now seventy-year-olds were approaching or had reached sixty, we contemplated retirement in the next few years. Some years earlier, we had looked at the interest rates that hovered around ten per cent and thought, well, if I can stick $500,000 in the bank and get ten per cent return on that, it will have a nice little annual income.

Since then, interest rates have stayed historically low and the lowest ever rate recently bottomed at 0.1%. Thanks, banks – 0.1% interest. If we had deposited $500,000, which is really a dream rather than a reality, we would now be yielding an annual income from that $500,000 of $5,000. If you want to lock your money away in a bank for three years – something we can ill afford, given that time is against us – then the best you can get is 3.25%. For two years, you'll get 2.5%. Whacko. That's $12,500 a year. If you gave all your money away and applied for a government pension, you'd receive roughly twice that. But that is pie in the sky.

As is the idea that we have sufficient income to invest in the share market, or the bond market, or any other market that wants us to give them our money for some small return. There are a lot of what they call 'products' out there. By products they mean financial schemes dreamed up to help you with your money. By calling them products, they let us believe we have something tangible that we can touch and smell. But we don't. Once they take our money, it can be very hard to get it back. Not hard in the sense that they won't give it to us, more the fact that they put up so many hurdles that it's exhausting trying, so it becomes easier to give up and leave it where it is.

Try moving from one bank to another. You have your credit cards, your pension or other income being deposited, your savings account (try saving anything on a fixed income) and other things that they may have locked you in to over the years. You Bpay your electricity and water bills. To change banks, you'd need to reset all those things and change all the direct deposits and get new credit cards. All too hard for an old bloke. So despite your bank sticking images of young people from mixed-race families on their websites and acknowledging LGBTQI folk, and using funny pronouns to describe their biological sex, which you may or may not agree with, you know if you go to the alternative they'll have the same stuff because all banks are corporate and all corporates need to play the game and make profits for their shareholders.

If you're a pensioner, you don't need to concern yourself with any of this. Your pension will arrive in your bank account, you'll invest it in food, clothing, medication and housing – what used to be called keeping yourself warm, dry and fed – and if there's any left, which is doubtful, you can have a few beers.

If you're not and you have a marginally better income that allows you to do things like go on holiday or buy a new car every few years, then you're doing well and you probably have what they call a mixed income. You probably have superannuation income, a share portfolio, or a property portfolio or fixed-term investments such as property trusts. The question for you is whether or not your income will last as long as you will. There's a deeper question for you and that is, who do you trust? Do you trust your bank? Do you trust your superannuation fund? Are you a self-funded retiree? Where do you need to invest in the next few years to keep yourself afloat to enjoy what life is providing?

One of the problems for us is that many seventy-year-olds are living in houses that are now worth far more than we paid for them. Quite a lot more, in fact, so that if we sold, we'd be rolling in dough and we could live the dream of taking up residence in the Savoy in London, eating every meal out and drinking champagne before breakfast and playing golf in Scotland. We tend not to do that, though. We tend to cling to the asset we have because if we sell, the government will add it to our income and start taxing us on it. At present, it's tax-free but at some point in the future, without wishing to be seen as a curmudgeon, one or other of the major parties will be in power and think, 'You know what, if we tax the family home, it could be a nice little earner for us', then all hell will break loose and housing prices will crash, but on a positive note, interest rates might go up.

What if we sell the house and downsize? There are plenty of people out there who want us to do precisely that – sell the big empty house and move into a flat or, better still, a 'granny flat' behind the house our children live in. A granny flat. Well named. Governments have even changed legislation so their developer mates can offer you the opportunity to build a house and a granny flat brand-new so that you can have somewhere nice to live out your dotage with family nearby so you can look after your grandchildren. Bloody buggery to that. Governments, developers and your own family are in cahoots with their hands in your pockets before you even start dribbling and talking to yourself.

If you're not the recipient of a government pension, then the question is how much do you need to live day-to-day or week-to-week? Paying the bills – the power and water, the insurance, the car rego, the rates (if you own a house) is your first priority. I find that what comes in each month also goes out. There's nothing extra once you've paid all the bills and bought food. How many things do you need to prioritise?

If you attend your church service on a regular basis, how much do you give? Fifty? Twenty? Five dollars? Nothing if you don't have it. If you're a member of your local club, you pay an annual fee. You also pay to have your car serviced and your rego checked each year. God forbid if something goes wrong and you need to spend money on a new fridge, washing machine or television. You can get some pretty cheap TVs these days but you still have to have the money coming in for that to happen.

You go up to the club once or twice a week at happy hour so you can have a few sherbets with your mates. What about bunging twenty in the pokies? See if you can win back some of what you've kept the club alive with over the years. No such luck. Twenty. Gone. Kids' and grandkids' birthdays, wives' birthdays, petrol, a new pair of pyjamas, all cost you. Don't bother looking over the horizon to that couple of weeks up the coast fishing. And don't even let your mind wander to that tinnie you always wanted. Now that you have a fixed income with no prospect of supplementing it, that boat has sailed. That's why there are a lot of old codgers dithering around Marine Rescue bases up and down the coast, or pottering in State Emergency Services; they get to drive someone else's boat. But they don't get to fish, so it's really no compensation.

The one question that remains in all this is how do we sustain ourselves with enough money coming in to stay alive for as long as we expect without falling on the public purse? I have a mate who's in that predicament. He's not quite seventy and he needs to work for a few more years so that he can stay living in his own house, run his car and accumulate enough so that when the odometer clocks seventy he won't have the anxiety of being skint, busted flat in Baton Rouge. At sixty-seven, he ought to have stopped working full time. Fortunately, he lobbed into a new job which was three days a week to begin then full-time. He's committed to three years, which I think is not only commendable it's absolutely fantastic that he feels he has come through quite a lot including a divorce and now feels capable of continuing to use his skills and expertise in a field that he loves. I have the greatest admiration for anyone who can do that, especially as he's all the things that everyone today blames for all the problems of the past, present and future: in other words, he's an old white man. Good luck to him, I say. And if he needs it, I'll give him any support I can. As long as he doesn't ask for money.

Pride & Prejudice

There's a lot of public acknowledgement of how proud we are of something or other. Corporations are proud supporters of inclusivity. Indigenous Australians are proud to be members of their tribal 'people'. Indigenous Canadians are proud to be part of their history as Metic and Inuit. First Nations people of the United States are proud of their existence and people who live in Cornwall in the south-west of England are proud to call themselves Cornish.

My father saw service in World War II and, some years ago, I was asked by someone if I was proud of him. I wasn't sure how to answer, as I'd never thought of being proud of him. He was my father and he did what was expected of him. He didn't seek glory or public displays of affection or admiration (nor did he seek them privately), so it would never have occurred to me to be proud of him. He was in fact a humble man who never actively sought recognition.

On another occasion, I did some repair work on a deck for a bloke. He was old and he watched me throughout. When it was finished, he said, 'Now that's a job you can be proud of.' Again, I had no expectation of being proud, or of seeking to have someone say that I ought to be proud; it was just a job that needed to be done.

So what is pride and should we have it or not by the time we reach seventy? Equally important is the question of whether someone who is proud fosters in others some sort of prejudice.

In one sense, this can be explained by the act of giving. When was the last time you offered to buy someone a cup of coffee, for example, and they accepted? The next time you saw them, you were disappointed because they failed to remember or to reciprocate your act of generosity. Imagine if that happened in a pub. You're in a shout and the last bloke leaves before his shout. It happened to me once after a press conference. There were four of us and we decided to catch up over a couple of ales and discuss the event. Three of us shouted four schooners then the fourth bloke up and says he has to go. One of the others, a belligerent bloke a few years older than us, said very stridently, 'Righto, that's no problem. Just leave your money on the table.' It didn't happen and that was the last we ever saw of the miserable fella.

This sort of thing often happens with younger men. I recall one bloke who got away with saying he had left his wallet at home once, then twice, but never again. His mates made it clear he was no longer invited. And rightly so. But in the case of the generosity of spirit in buying someone a coffee, is there, or should there be, an expectation that at a later date they'll come good? Not really. Unless you made it clear that you would buy this time and they could buy next. They may decide not to enter into the transaction. If you feel like being generous, does that mean the person you're being generous towards should feel the same? Your generosity of spirit is up to you. I'd like to think that the next time I would remember and offer to buy the coffee but what if there is no next time? Or the expanse of time between is so great that you forget? There have been a couple of instances when I have paid for lunch with the expectation that the next time the other party would offer to pay. I'm still waiting.

When we're generous and receive nothing in return, small prejudices begin to surface. Like the bloke who walked away rather than paying for a few beers. We very quickly develop a prejudice against them. We tend to look at each other so that what we imagine becomes what we see. Some years ago, I was asked, when talking about a third person, if he was someone I would want to be in the trenches with. It was a war metaphor; you needed to be able to trust and rely on the bloke next to you when the firing and shelling started. It was an unusual question to put but in this example the person in question was not someone the other bloke would want to be in the trenches with, it turned out. He didn't trust him or something like that, but the irony was that the bloke asking the question turned out to be exactly the same. When push came to shove, he wasn't reliable.

But things like reliability and trust are not what seventy-year-olds have come to believe others will provide. We've been around too long to believe politicians and it's even difficult to believe your general practitioner these days. They like to ask you what's wrong rather than doing their jobs and diagnosing you for themselves. The trouble is, push no longer comes to shove, so there's no test to prove reliability or truth or trust. Everywhere you turn, your prejudices are confirmed. Which is perhaps why very small tribal groups of older men stick pretty much to who they know rather than venturing to engage with wider society. You know those blokes at the table of knowledge in the back bar on Thursday arvo will have your back. And you'll have theirs.

There may have been an incident or event that cemented that trust but more often than not it's simply the act of being thrown together in some country town or coastal retirement village that builds the trust. And your previous working life. Don't trust the seventy-year-old retired public servant from Canberra. Trust the retired seventy-year-old boilermaker from Penrith. Don't rely on the seventy-year-old retired chalky from Sydney to tell the truth. Rely on the seventy-year-old retired dairy farmer from Victoria. God love 'em.

While undertaking a bit of research for this sketch, I came across a bizarre use of the word pride. It was on the side of a package of duck pancakes. After the fashion of a lot of packaged products these days, it required self-affirmation. The manufacturer advertised itself on the side of the box – without a hint of irony – as an Australian family-owned company that takes pride in the welfare of its ducks. It added that it was based in Victoria and that its ducks have constant access to a nutritious grain-based diet. We can assume the constant access ceases once the duck's plucked, but it's the word pride that's of most interest. Is it similar in intent to the bloke who told me I'd done a job I could be proud of? I suspect there's more to it in that organisations compete so ferociously they've concluded that they don't need to align themselves with causes, all they need to do is use the words that will resonate with their customers. But who in their right mind reads all the words on a box of dead duck? If it tells us what's in the box and it's the right price, bingo.

Businesses succumb to pressure very easily. It doesn't take much for them to adopt new slogans that have some parallel with activist causes. This is known as 'purpose marketing'. It appeals to emotions but also to controversy which is designed to engage Millennials who reject traditional advertising messages. In a market where being socially aware or 'woke' becomes important, it may be that the actual product or the message itself is distilled so that it's no longer relevant. To take pride in a manufacturing process or a scientific discovery is not the same as taking pride in the welfare of a duck. One would assume that the welfare of the duck is a given, at least until it's slaughtered and stuck in a box with pancakes and hoisin sauce.

But let me go back to a game of rugby league in which the Kayo commentators got so worked up because, they pronounced, it was an absolute corker of a game in which both teams fought it out for eighty minutes. The best game they had seen all season. Wait. Is the NRL a professional 'corporatised' game? Is it not a given that every team will run on to the field each week and play to their absolute best? The captain of the winning side, when talking after the game, was asked if he was proud of his team. He said yeah, it was good to take the win but it was going to be equally good to have the weekend off and have a few beers and kick back. Again, wait. Are these blokes not paid between $500,000 and $1 million to play eighty minutes flat-out football once a week? The losing captain on the night made all the right remarks concluding with the need for his team to learn their lessons and work harder next time. It was another one of those rehearsed lines we've come to expect from players, and if there's a win, then they're always proud of the effort their team made on the day.

Almost serendipitously, I discovered a book of poetry: the last published works of Vincent Buckley. In it, I came across 'Holiness of the Meat Trade', in which Buckley concludes by lamenting the loss of calves in his youth in the sale yards, his calves 'my hand cupping their soft chins / my arms about their necks / glaring about me, tight with alarm / as they're herded, mad with pride / as the bidding moves up'. Mad with pride. An interesting uncommon phrase and not one that you might associate with cows and calves. They were also, he writes, tight with alarm, which it's reasonable to assume given their circumstances in the sale yard. Mad with pride is another thing altogether. Mad with power, mad with rage, mad with love are all in common usage. I suspect mad with pride deserves a resurgence.

Negotiate & Navigate

This one is the biggy. What it means is you're at an age where you need – and I say need rather than want because you don't want to have to do it – you need to negotiate everything. You can't drive down the street without negotiating your way around people running on the road rather than the footpath. It's you who must navigate around them not them getting out of the way for you. It wasn't always difficult.

There was a time when you could do five hundred things in a single day. They may not have been earth-shattering things but you could do them mostly without having to think too much about it. I needed to go to the local pathology lab to have blood taken. My doctor (although she has only an undergraduate degree, I'll still call her doctor, out of respect), suggested it was time to test my PSA. We all have that now. Blood tests for prostate problems, that is. PSA means prostate specific antigen. Blood shows what's going on with your prostate. It used to be different. Your doctor, generally male, would get you to lie on your side with your dacks down while he stuck his finger up your clacker. Apparently, this was the way to go – he could feel if your prostate was enlarged without the need for blood samples. And he always had a joke about a second opinion, while holding up his index and middle finger together. Or about the worst thing that could happen, doing a prostate test right before lunch and the latex glove breaks.

Women doctors seem to have changed the way we do things. They're not real keen to do the finger test, or, as one bloke remarked, if you have to do it, find a Chinese woman doctor with small fingers. But that's not the point. It took me a week to go in to the lab, not because I was busy with other things, although I was for a couple of days. It was more about the fasting and then getting myself up the street. Until recently, I took the dog for a walk most mornings between five thirty and six thirty. We did around five kilometres. More recently, I've stopped walking early, promising to do it later in the day because getting up and making a coffee and going back to bed was a softer option. Well, now I don't feel like walking anywhere. I blame the corona booster because it laid me low for a few weeks but I haven't got the energy to start the early mornings again. Which brings me back to the blood.

Once, I would have jumped out of bed, had the big drink of water and walked the kilometre to the lab, done the blood thing then back home for a big brekkie. Instead, I found myself worrying about whether I should walk, or drive, or drive partway and walk. The drive bit is easy, except that you then get caught up in peak-hour traffic which lasts for more than three hours and it takes longer to drive home than it would to walk. I chose to drive to the railway station, park and walk the rest of the way, which was about 400 metres. In the rain.

But I began to get anxious about getting a parking spot, about going an extra hundred metres to cross the road at the lights or to scoot across the traffic, about how many other people would be there, about how long I'd have to wait. All the crappy things that never entered my mind when I was younger. Then when I got in to the waiting room, I worried that someone else would get called before my number and what I would do about it if it did. It didn't. And I didn't trip over on the wet road and get squashed by an Australian of Chinese heritage driving an Audi SUV. I got my blood taken by a nice woman of Chinese heritage, and walking back to the car I looked over the road to the bakery and thought how well a sticky bun would go with my coffee when I got home. But there were three people in there, it was raining and I would have had to either go further to the traffic lights and walk back on the other side, or dodge across the traffic. I convinced myself that the two slices of week-old raisin bread would toast nicely and proceeded to walk on in the rain, got in the car and drove home.

The point is not that I physically achieved what I set out to achieve – have blood taken so that my doctor can tell me my prostate is enlarged – the point is I went through more mental anxiety than I ever needed to but I couldn't help myself. It was as if my brain had decided to go into risk assessment mode and to analyse and categorise every minute detail of what could go wrong. But it's not only the 'what could go wrong' scenario. It's also the 'want to but can't find the energy to do it' one.

If my mother were alive, she would have been so for a hundred years. She's not, of course, having died at sixty-seven. She was born a hundred years ago in a town in south-western NSW on the Murrumbidgee river. So I had the bright idea of celebrating her birth by driving to the town for a few days and visiting the hospital to pay my respects. Here's where inspiration meets fatigue. Nice idea but up go the hurdles and barriers. Let's list them as they surfaced.

1. Too soon after the Omicron variant. Not good to go anywhere yet as there might be other variants around the corner.

2. Petrol prices. With 98RON almost $3 a litre, a trip there and back would have an estimated cost of $300 calculated at ten litres each hundred kilometres.

3. Add accommodation and meals and things start to look a bit less enticing than first imagined.

What then are the alternatives, if any? The simplest thing would be to send the nursing staff a nice card with a message of thanks for bringing my mother into the world. After all, without them, my grandmother might have had to give birth beside a stump or a clump of mimosa along a dirt track, which was pretty much what the next best thing might have looked like. But it wasn't them, was it? The doctors and nurses who worked there a hundred years ago are in the same place as my mother. Which brings me back to the point. My brain starts thinking well, you know, would anyone there actually care about some old bloke sending them a card to say his mother was born there? Probably not. Very probably not. So what would be the point, I tell myself. Besides, do I really want to have to go somewhere to buy a card, then find a stamp for the envelope and then post it all? Do I put a return contact on it? How will I know they got it?

The alternative is to send them an email. That's easy. 'Dear Hospital Person, My mother was born at your hospital a hundred years ago but she's been dead now for more than thirty years so it's all pretty irrelevant except that I'm thinking about her and how she must have been all those years ago. What was it like being born there? How long did she and her mother stay? What was it like taking a small baby girl thirty miles southwest of town along a dirt road to a small railway siding where her father was stationed? How did she and her elder sister survive those first years of their lives in a two-room weatherboard house where there were two peppercorn trees, a few outbuildings and a railway siding and platform, three other similar houses and a post office? I know you don't have any answers for me. I don't really want any. I write simply to say thank you to your fellow medical staff for bringing her into the world a hundred years ago.'

The idea of sending a brief email doesn't really satisfy a desire to celebrate the occasion. The question is not so much about a need to recognise the significant milestone as it is to honour that person. And it's bound up in more complex questions about the significance of memory, the importance of recognising loss, the virtue in maintaining core values and not letting things slip away without doing something about them.

Some years ago, I spoke with a man in Canberra who, for many years, had maintained a record of all the people who had sprung from the union of his ancestors' Second Fleet soldier Edward Field and convicted woman Betty Mitchell. I had recently visited the old Castlereagh cemetery where Edward and Betty are buried. It was in such a state of disrepair that I was keen to vent my anger on the local council and the state government over their appalling maintenance of such a historic site. Colin Field said he was not surprised. He said the local council wanted the site to go away because it wasn't interested in maintaining old graves that had links to the colonial era.

Such is the state of affairs that by taking the easy path, the email for example, things do slip and once they slip they eventually disappear from view. And once they disappear from view, they're lost to memory and thence, without much of a struggle, lost forever.

(I did send the email and, as expected, I received no reply.)

Change Up & Change Down

For me, the date of my turning seventy was not as significant as I would have liked it to be. I was in a coronavirus lockdown which, if you put it to the tune of 'Alabama High Test', might sound okay but in reality it was the opposite of okay. There was a planned seventieth birthday party which did not happen. There were a couple of bottles of single malt from unusual sources, sources which were, I would say, unexpected. And much appreciated. Then there were those that were expected, or at least anticipated, that never eventuated. Nothing mattered in isolation and lockdown except lowering the risk of catching Covid-19. As we know, however, this was not to be. Nothing changed for a few months. Lockdown ceased but there was still a hesitancy to become more socially involved. My birthday was in July but it was not until almost nine months later that the subtle shifts that had been taking place became more obvious and far, far more challenging.

The subtle shifts involved conscious decisions. To continue with a regular event, to continue to participate in a regular event or not. Some of the things were simple enough, a regular lawn bowls game, a golf game, a regular Lifeline shift as a crisis supporter. Covid-19 took the regularity and shoved it sideways. There was no longer any regular activity. If it was a time for reflection, then it was a tough way to do it.

But out of that reflection came the clarity that said hey, wait a minute, what are these things that you continue to do when you have a limited time in which to do them? What are the things you really want to do if you survive Covid-19?

Some of them will never be the same again. I can't imagine long-haul flights to Europe or America. I get claustrophobic on planes anyway, so this has been a really good opportunity to say, well, there's really nowhere in the world I want to go anyway and I don't see myself sitting on a plane for twenty-four hours wearing a mask even if I could afford to travel business class. So that bird has flown and what a relief. I have had the joy of playing golf in Scotland but do I need it again? I have climbed mountains in New Zealand and Scotland but will never be fit enough to do it again, so here's the perfect excuse not to. All of that is now in the past. I can reflect on it if I wish, but I can also let it lie. It can remain in the past.

What about golf and bowls? Do I enjoy them? I enjoy the actual playing but the crap that goes on and that attaches to them, the need to always be competitive, to strive for being better at it, that's also for the birds, or at least younger players. At seventy, we still get sucked into that vortex of competition without knowing how to get out of it. Well, we can also set those things aside for the time being. We may come back to them later but right now they are off the table. No deal. In fact, I've taken everything off the table for the immediate future. Even walking the dog in the early morning. Now I find it much more satisfying to take a cup of coffee back to bed and read *The Spectator* until I feel like getting up.

The one thing that I will continue is my Lifeline commitment. It's not something I thought would be top of mind but numerous events over the past years, Covid-19, floods, bushfires have made me more attuned to the vast number of individuals in our society who are in desperate need of someone to talk to. And if as part of that I can give someone with suicidal ideation the possibility of hope, then it doesn't get any better than that.

The difficulty with changing, either up or down when you get to seventy, is that some things refuse to flow along with you. When I sleep, I dream and in those dreams I'm never an old man. I'm not conscious of how old I actually am in the dreams but I know that others in my dreams are significantly younger than seventy. Sometimes, they're people I know but more often they're imaginary; and the actions and events in the dreams are imaginative. It may be that I dream of a relationship. It may be a dream of a woman. Sometimes, the dream is very clear yet when I wake there's nothing to tie it to anything that I am now. Or was in the past. It's as if the imagined person is imagined in some other youthful dimension which includes me. Does it mean I'm trying to change down rather than up? Does it mean I'm attempting to move back rather than forward because there's less life in front and more behind (unless I plan to live to 140; then it would be about the same in front as at back).

Here I think a baseball analogy is a good explanation. A pitcher changes up by throwing a slow ball with the same motion that he throws a fast ball. The slow ball is thrown from further back in the hand, which releases it more slowly. This is a tactic meant to deceive the batter into making a strike at the ball before it reaches the plate.

In English usage, it also means to engage a higher gear but in American usage it means to make something different or to do something differently. Perhaps the new abnormal for the seventy-year-old might be to start throwing slow balls that look like fast balls, not to deceive anyone but to do it differently for ourselves.

The decision to change up is not an easy one and the place from which to start to change up is equally difficult. So many layers of existence need to be cut through. So much baggage needs to be chucked in the bin. Only then can you begin to grasp the significance of your actions. In front of you there will be a wide clear path. You can decide which way you want to go. You can decide when you want to go. There are no constraints. Except possibly the financial constraint to being and going. We will cover this in detail in the concluding chapter.

For now, what becomes important is to look for meaning in everything you do as a seventy-year-old. Look for the meaning of meaning in it, which is to say look beneath and above the meaning to see what really drives your present existence. What is it that keeps you anchored to all the things you have done in the past, all the things you can no longer do but still think that one day you might again be able to? All the things that have ceased to exist for you yet you keep mementos of them, shrines, in your shed or your garage.

When did you last use that old climbing rope you bought in 1978? Once or twice? In 1979. It has taken up space in your garage for forty-four years. No, wait. You used it in 1986 to remove a tree stump. And what about the three bikes hanging on the side wall? Tyres perished, mildew on the seat, oxidised chain and brake cables. Last used? Probably 1990.

Without wishing to put too fine a point on it, perhaps it's time to remove the physical baggage and then, with a bit of luck, the mental baggage that constrains your future well-being will also be removed.

It Is What It Is

This is one of the stupidest expressions ever uttered. Most often, it comes from the mouths of thirty-somethings who have been dudded in some way by someone – possibly No and Sum. I have heard it in different situations: a young bloke who didn't make the grade in Aussie rules football, a woman whose house got burned in a bushfire; and a man who claimed he was being evicted from public housing so a block of flats could be built on the site. Another late-thirtyish woman used it in answer to a question about a reduction in her work.

There's nowhere to go when someone makes the statement *it is what it is*, no continued discussion or conversation. It's a blunt instrument which is meant to shut down any further conversation. It can be used as such when someone doesn't want to talk about what has happened to them, doesn't want to look more closely at the situation confronting them.

Unlike *Que sera sera*, or *Che sera sera*, *it is what it is* claims nothing. *Que sera sera* means whatever will be will be, as it was sung by Doris Day, but whatever will be will be after everything has been done to make sure that whatever will be, will be.

It is what it is is a cop out, a validation of failure. There's nothing remotely philosophical about the phrase, to accept failure is to accept defeat. I have not yet heard a seventy-year-old use the phrase. Failure's not a concept that sits easily with those of us who have navigated three score and ten. Defeat is something that happens only after every avenue of hope has been explored. I can't imagine confronting the end of life with something as banal as *it is what it is*. There is always hope.

For many, that hope at the hour of death lies in the resurrection of the body and the life everlasting. For others, it's the separation of the soul from the body and the wait for judgement. Boundless trivia assault those who venture too close to pop culture. 'Go for it' is another. Go for what? 'We need the rain' might be one that could be removed from the lexicon, at least until the next drought.

Others such as 'the new normal', and 'social distancing', have surfaced with the outbreak of the coronavirus pandemic but one of the best and silliest is the single word 'unprecedented'. As we seventy-year-olds know, nothing is unprecedented unless history is forgotten. There is a precedent for everything. A precedent can be described as an action or event that has taken place and can be used as an exemplar when similar circumstances arise. To say that a flood is unprecedented or that a pandemic is unprecedented is nonsense. It's an attempt to deny history.

What the user may mean is that the event or action is large or more significant than previous events or actions, or indeed, smaller, but there is always a precedent. If you live for seventy years, then there's probably nothing in your future that will be unprecedented. Except death. Everything you have achieved, all the failures, all the successes have precedents.

What are some of the things you've done in life? As seventy-year-old men, we can reflect upon our lives – the achievements, the failures – with certainty that most of them we will never need to do again. We can wake to a new morning each day and know that we never have to compete, we never have to win an argument, we never have to prove to anyone that we're worthy. We've done it all, or most of it, and whether we've done it well or poorly is irrelevant. Those coming behind us are still to do the things we have done. How they do them is up to them. I suspect a lot of them will achieve nowhere near what we achieved in the same way that we have not achieved what our fathers achieved.

On the other hand, they will achieve a great deal more because the technology, the know-how, the physicality will alter so that they can run faster, dig deeper and climb higher but, more generally, most of the things we have done they will do in exactly the same way. They won't find new ways to make babies. Or eat food. Or read books. Or in fact play golf. They may hit their tee shots further and as the technology of club design improves they may find more interesting ways to approach a green but ultimately, unless the rules change, they'll still have to putt out to finish the hole.

At seventy, it's not what it is. We have lived in a world that has altered inexorably from the one that emerged at the end of World War II. It's different. It's exciting. It's full of change but it remains the same. We can watch without needing to be involved or to make comment. We can, within the limits of physical and financial well-being, do, as John Denver wrote, 'whatever you want to do, wherever you want to go, it's up to you'. And it never, ever has to be what it is. If generations of men had succumbed, then poet Dylan Thomas would never have written, 'Do not go gentle into that good night / Old age should burn and rave at close of day / Rage, rage against the dying of the light.' What if instead, the Welsh poet had sat quietly under milk wood and written, 'It is what it is'? Where would we all be now? Well, we won't be around by the time the generation who have embraced this nonsense make it to seventy, if they actually do. More likely, they'll give up the ghost much earlier. So continue to rage, rage against the dying of the light.

Ratbags

The older you get, the easier it seems to be to deal with ratbags. When you were young, there were always blokes who would goad you into something or other whether it was on the footy field or the cricket pitch and you'd find yourself being sucked into getting angry which, in turn, took your eye off the ball. It was and still is a common tactic, known as sledging, but there are other ways to make you mad and divert you from the goal of winning.

One tactic, rather than to make a specific direct derogatory comment about an individual, is the aside. An aside is a remark that might be made more generally which in the intensity of the game is enough to put you off your stride. As you get older, these asides become more common because they form a large part of the machinery of defeat. A competitor knows they can't beat you, so they say things – or, equally, don't say things when they ought to say something. This sounds a bit convoluted. Let me give you an example.

You're now seventy and have taken up the game of bowls. Most of the members of your club are decent chaps, happy to still be above ground. They enjoy their bowls and enjoy even more a couple of quiet ales at the end of a game. Some of the younger blokes like a drink during the game too. Then there will be the bloke who makes it his business to use tactics other than his game to try to put his opponent off. He's the bloke who walks from end to end without speaking to his opponent, stands on the centre line behind the head to distract his opponent, and refuses to provide clarification on minor matters such as sharing the score or marking a 'toucher'. These blokes are everywhere and can make your life miserable if you let them. The secret is in not letting them get under your skin.

I know of a man who's being constantly harassed by his neighbours. He owns a factory which has a common driveway to his neighbour's trucking business. His neighbour frequently and consciously parks his trucks either across the drive or in the drive so the factory owner can't access his property. He has tried reasoning with them, which failed, so he took them to court which, as you can guess, exacerbated the issue. His neighbours became abusive and threatening to the point where it affected his mental and physical well-being. He thought he would have to sell his factory and leave. Which may have been the point of the neighbour's bad behaviour in the first place. He was unsure. He made a life-changing decision. Rather than say anything, which only antagonised them, he decided to be nice. So each morning when he arrived, he called out 'Good morning.' At first they slung abuse and told him to get fucked. After a few months of morning greetings and of doing nothing when they parked their trucks in the drive, one or two members of the family began to say hello back.

He said the problem was still there because the matriarch was the main contributor to the abuse but after a while the sons started to nod and wave back and eventually they began parking their trucks on the street instead of in his drive. He said it was one of the hardest things he has ever had to do, to be nice to people who were being pricks. He also admitted that before he began being nice, he was at the end of his rope and had begun looking to the Bible for answers, something he did when he was younger. He didn't go so far as to say it was some faith in Jesus that had helped him through his crisis but he did acknowledge that he found he could get on with his life when he stopped letting the antagonists get to him.

He still has problems with his neighbours and admits that it will probably never stop completely but at least he feels he can get on with things because he hasn't allowed them to get into his head. He also said that he got some satisfaction from reading that cricketer Shane Warne had said he was able to take a lot of wickets not because he was a spectacular bowler but because he could get inside a batsman's head.

This brings us back to the bowls game where the antagonist is doing the same thing – trying to get inside an opponent's head. You might think that by the time you get to seventy, this would not be something you would bother with. Too many other things to contend with in life, so why bother trying to be mean-spirited. Well, this is how some men behave all their lives. They begin with mean spirits and they never stop. Too much salt on the liver, I remember someone saying, but it's more than that. These men generally lead unfulfilled lives. They probably retired too early, had jobs with very little satisfaction, or something simpler; they're just pricks and have been all their lives. They get their kicks from seeing someone else suffer. Much like the factory owner's next-door truckers. When you find yourself becoming irritated by something one of these pricks is trying to do to you, tell yourself that it is after all only a bowls match, or a game of golf. If you laugh it off, that in itself will get to the prick, who senses he is unable to rattle you. And once he's unable to get inside your head, you have the game in the bag.

Coronavirus

I had no plans to include this deadly virus in this book but there I was, narrowly and slowly recovering from a bout. It's a bit like a really, really bad dose of influenza, the experts say, with a few nasty additions such as a powerful aching head, joint pain, an itchy rash and fatigue so bad you never want to get out of bed. It's also the fear that has been implanted in you by your various governments that makes it much worse.

Before you get it, as a seventy-year-old male, you think you might be in reasonable physical and mental condition. Let me tell you the first twenty-four hours with this virus and you can kiss goodbye to any sense of both. It attacks your lungs, making breathing fearfully difficult, but it also attacks your brain and your limbs so that you feel less like a seventy-year-old and more like ninety.

If you're a seventy-year-old without any support, say from family or friends or carers, then you need to think very carefully before you go anywhere you are likely to contract this virus. When you test positive, you're legally bound to register with your provincial government. That means you tell them you have it and they send you back an anonymous cold text message saying you must stay isolated for the next seven days.

Well, let me tell you, and anyone who's had it would have to agree, there's no way you're going anywhere because you can barely get out of bed for the first week. The idea of driving your car, or walking somewhere is out of the question. Not only do you have difficulty moving around, you struggle to link two thoughts together. Every ounce of strength is channelled into staying alive. This is not a joke. When you're in the grip of the virus, the only thing that you think about is whether or not you'll die. Whether you'll stop breathing. Or, if you have a weak heart, whether it will stop beating.

Don't pay too much attention to those who shrug it off as a bad cold. That bravado does no one any good. It's a dangerous virus that can kill you. At the same time, the fear you have of it can be divided between what you were told by governments and what you now know yourself. Your own fear is justified. You're seventy years old. You already have aches and pains. You have, as we have mentioned above, prostate problems, joint problems, reduced kidney and liver function. In fact, if you get it, there's a strong chance it will kill you. But then you've had your vaccinations and that ought to keep you safe. Or that's what they told you when you had them.

But here you are with the virus ravaging your poor old body and you wonder how, if you survive, you'll get back to some sense of normality. Well, it may take some time, if ever, for you to become the person you still want to be. Don't rush.

There's much talk of 'long' Covid, symptoms that can stay with you and cause problems months from when you thought you were over it. In England, a survey of positive patients found ten per cent had at least one symptom three months after initial infection. Symptoms included extreme fatigue, shortness of breath, heart palpitations, memory loss and poor concentration, and joint or muscle pain.

Most government organisation say well, golly gosh, there you go, you have long Covid. Stay home and don't give it to others. The Australian College of GPs provides additional advice, which is to stop smoking. That's about as useful as a pocket in a singlet. A bit like having to fill in gender equality forms which ask if you're a male, then ask you to tick the box if you're pregnant.

The GP college also has advice about prioritising tasks. If you can't do them all because of fatigue, they suggest asking a friend or family member to do them for you. One has to question if these people are living in a parallel universe where everyone has friends and everyone has family just down the street who can drop everything and come to your aid. Perhaps they do, or they have the capacity to pay others to do things for them. For the majority of us, especially males over seventy, there's a good chance we're living alone, our family's off in other parts of the country or world, if we have any, and our friends are in the same boat as us. Again, if we have any.

If you live alone and you're in your seventies, then you're probably in deep trouble if you get the virus. There's plenty of stuff online that tells you what to do to 'stay connected' and other well-meaning but pious advice to 'reach out' to people you may have lost contact with. And be open to new invitations from people you feel comfortable with. Well, what the f*^k? Here you probably are, starting to feel like rubbish, your temperature's gone through the roof, your throat's doing razor blades and you can't breath. Right, you say. Time to be open to new invitations.

While I was in the grip of the virus, one of the things that lessened my fears was the mates who were there if I needed them. I'm one of the lucky ones. I texted them when symptoms came on and told them what I thought was about to unleash. I'd fought it for a week while my wife went down with it, so I was already in isolation. One mate who lives nearby offered to shop, another two further afield offered the same or anything else needed, even though it was a holiday weekend at the time, and my daughter, who lives 300 kilometres away, said she would come and look after us.

Not everyone has such rewarding relationships. The text message from the mate up the street was enough for me to know that someone was there. But what if there's no one? What of you other seventy-year-olds or older men, who have no one upon whom you can rely? I know a few. Some will get the virus, suffer terribly for a week or ten days, then begin to improve. They may have become dehydrated and need medical attention but they will shove their way through.

Others will succumb and die. They may lie in bed for days unable to breathe. There are men who live such isolated lives that it may be a long time before they're missed. What advice does the government have for them? Perhaps they would tell them, in the next life, to call for an ambulance. What if they have no telephone? Unheard of in the twenty-first century, right? Wrong. Politicians will put on sad faces and say how tragic such circumstances are. Charitable organisations will seek more funding, arguing that they can better assist those living in isolation and loneliness. But in the end, those old men will simply die.

My mind wandered during the peak of the virus to the possibility of not surviving. It was not a pretty thought but it was one that needed to be had. It was as if everything that had gone before rolled up into a ball and disappeared in a puff of smoke. The past ceased to exist. And there was no future, only the possibility of ceasing to exist also. It was as if my mind had disengaged so that I could use every ounce of what was left of strength to fight the virus.

I pumped paracetamol into me every four hours to attempt to numb the throat soreness and sat over a Vick's Vaporub bowl of hot water to try to open my airways so I could breathe. The respiratory blockage was the worst part of it. the joint pain and the sore throat and head combined, but I could tolerate them. It was the lungs that worried me. Everything I had read and every health boffin on television had me already dead if my lungs collapsed. This added anxiety didn't help. Had I read the College of GPs' advice beforehand, I would have seen that they recommend speaking to my GP about breathing control exercises and to remain calm, as stress and anxiety can increase my heart rate, which makes me breathless. My goodness. What sensible advice.

As a manifesto, this book is about declaring my intentions and views rather than providing advice. But if I had to offer advice on how to deal with Covid, if you get it when you're over seventy and alone, I would say be prepared and obtain a personal alarm or carry a cheap burner phone with you at all times and call 000 if you feel it's threatening your life. You might also consider having a conversation with a one or other of the support agencies, Lifeline or Mensline, who can arrange a welfare check for you. Despite what governments and politicians tell you, you are alone.

Forgiveness

If you're a Christian, forgiveness is something you learn and apply throughout your life. It becomes more important in your later adult life, much as it does in your childhood, because harbouring grudges or bad feelings does nothing except make you continually bitter and twisted.

As a seventy-year-old male, you will have been confronted throughout your life by multiple offenders. Since the 1960s, a variety of offenders have been having a crack at men often for the simple reason that they are men. Or they were boys becoming men, which was, to the offenders, the same terrible thing. Now they refer to it as toxic masculinity. But who are *they*? Well, they're anyone who decides that white men are fair game; historically, the offenders against men have been feminists and lefties. By that, I mean a conservative man has, during the past forty or fifty years, become fair game for other men on the progressive left, and women who call themselves feminists.

Think of the number of times you've been hard done by during your working life. Or the number of times you've been shafted by feminists or lefties because you were perceived to be not of the same political persuasion as them. It happens to women too but this book is about men, particularly those in and around seventy who have been around long enough to experience subversive attacks on them because they're men.

I know of a case in which a Millennial woman took on a difficult task left by another slightly older feminist. The feminist had left her job and made calculated errors so that the organisation would fail. The Millennial woman came in, took over and kept the place going. This was too much for the feminist, who the Millennial thought was her friend. The feminist went around town bad-mouthing the Millennial.

This is a typical example of someone deciding she will get you because you're good at what you do. You're professional and treat people with respect and dignity but for the angry feminist that's not the result she wanted. She will spend a lot of time and energy until the poor Millennial is brought down to her level. The Millennial still forgives the feminist and cannot understand how she could cut off her friendship of a few years.

It's easy to understand if you know how these people work. They're generally not very good at what they do and they hate with a passion anyone who is any good. This used to be called cultural cringe but I suspect it's no longer due to a lack of culture. It has become a deep hatred of everything directly or indirectly associated with conservative institutions and society.

My own experiences have occurred within the confines of those institutions now occupied by the left – universities, publishing houses and some sections of the media. My career took numerous twists and turns, some up dry gullies, others across vast open plains where you could see forever. The dry gully I would associate with a low point from which there was always recovery because nothing is so bad that you cannot get back to where you want to be. Some of the dry gullies had sheer rock walls at their ends so I had to retrace and find an alternative route. One of them was so dry and so steep I had to change direction completely, change up and onto the next level, which brought me a lot of satisfaction but ultimately led me into a morass of leftist feminist anger that I did not know how to manage or confront.

Let's say that I now understand it all and forgive many of those who were the perpetrators of the offences against me. I am not, nor was I ever, a victim or a survivor of these offences. To be so is to assume some sort of relationship with the offender. I was always able to walk away from the offender but sometimes I wish I had been forearmed so I could have at least defended myself. Most of the offences were attacks on me because I was a man. Many occurred in the last years of my working life at a leading university. A couple in particular stand out.

In 2007, I had two books published. At the same time, another person in the department in which I worked published a chapter in a book. The head of department, a feminist scholar made an occasion of the other person's book chapter, lauding it as exceptional and congratulating her, to which everyone in the meeting applauded and celebrated her achievement. As did I. But my two books got no mention.

A number of years and minor irritations later, the newly appointed head of the school in which the department sat had a mandate to clear out everyone who did not fit her agenda. I recall that one weak, sad little lecturer abruptly changed his research focus. He had previously taught something vague about twentieth-century literature. The head of school actively sought to denigrate my research and my teaching to the point where I complained to the dean of the faculty about her sexist and ageist behaviour. He did nothing. I went on stress leave and very soon after retired from that post. I saw no mileage in staying on and being subjected to abusive behaviour when I had done nothing to deserve it except to be a white male.

Other similar but less severe career experiences involved women in management positions attempting to lever me out of a job so they could install a woman.

The point of this is not that I'm bitter or angry. These things happen to all of us and if we live long enough, then we will have had similar experiences. On the other side of the angry feminist is the woman in a position of power who thinks she can act with impunity in her behaviour towards men. This is not new and a lot of men in positions of authority exercise their power very badly. Women can be just as sneaky.

When I began as a volunteer with a rescue organisation, I was one day in close quarters with a couple of others on the rescue vessel when a woman put her hand on my bottom. It was not a fleeting 'oops sorry lurched into you' moment, it was a lingering hand that did not get removed for a few seconds. I made no move to acknowledge it and she moved away. But she never let it go. When she was elected to a position of authority, she made sure I knew who she was. Her behaviour towards me altered. Nothing significant in this, I hear you mutter, and no, probably not, but if you get enough of these things going on for you, then at some stage you become a little bit sensitive to it all. The best thing is to let it go. After all, that's what the original Greek translation of forgiveness means – to let it go.

The Christian Lord's Prayer incants, 'Forgive us our trespasses as we forgive them who trespass against us', or, in a later translation, 'Forgive us our sins as we forgive those who sin against us.' Islamic teaching encourages forgiveness. A question raised in Jewish teaching is whether true forgiveness means the restoration of trust.

Forgiveness has the capacity to make us less stressed, less anxious and more well balanced than if we harbour anger and hatred of others. It's not easy to forgive. Think about the examples I've provided where there was a degree of offence against me, a degree of hatred and anger towards me because I was a competent man. If I had let a similar level of hatred and anger build in me, I would have been just like them and I would have exhausted a lot of energy in replying in kind. It took me a few years to let it go.

I still don't like what happened and some of the scenarios meant my career as an academic did not progress as far as it might have. But I like to think that all the dry gullies I went up and came back out of over the years allowed me to grasp the significance of forgiveness. It's a bit like the old Four and Twenty pie advertisement a few years back. Two blokes were sitting out on the job having a smoko, a nelly bligh in hand watching a couple of other blokes in a classy restaurant dressed in suits and ties. One of the tradies says to the other, 'Do you think they know what they're missin?' Precisely.

To forgive someone is not necessarily to have them know that they're forgiven. You don't need to go to the person responsible for the offence and tell them you forgive them. This is television-style crime drama. Sometimes, the person giving offence or trespassing against you is unaware that they have done so. You may feel your 'boundaries' have been breached or that someone has done something to 'trigger' a hurt. This is what political activists are very good at – pretending to be hurt by something and going out of their way to make sure the person or organisation causing the 'hurt' knows about it.

There was an example in a large law firm when the managing partner sent an email to all staff noting that an issue relating to the then federal attorney-general may have 'triggered a hurt' for the staff. The managing partner didn't last long after that. It made the firm look weak but it was the action of sending the email that played out the left's political activist agenda. It told them they were hurt and offended. The managing partner made an error of judgement in believing that the lawyers in the firm, because there were more than fifty per cent women, would agree with her assessment of the situation – that the attorney-general was a toxic male. Her dismissal from the firm proved this was not the case and that the firm itself was not a handmaiden of the left.

It's important for us as men to recognise that we can forgive transgressions and offences against us and that it assists us very ably in feeling less aggressive or angry. Some things, of course, are unforgivable but generally, letting go of something provides us with the freedom to see more clearly. We no longer need to think about the other thing or ever give it room to fester. To let it go is to let it go; to really let it go so that it never again enters our minds. Don't simply exchange it for another thought or problem. Let it go. It can be a bit like the times you feel like chucking stuff out of your shed or spare room but you don't because you'll have a need for that piece of timber or short piece of one-and-a-half-inch plastic pipe sometime in the future. Chuck 'em out. If they've been sitting there for more than two years and not been used, there's a pretty good chance you'll never use them in the remainder of your life. And if you need a similar item, go to the hardware shop and buy it.

You'll probably find you paid more for it twenty years ago than you will now. Use the old bracket or old broken circular saw as a metaphor. Forgive them for being rusty brackets and broken saws and chuck 'em. Clear the path to your future, however long or short that may be, but clear it so that you can invest your time in the things that are truly important to you. That's what being seventy is all about.

Death

By the time we make it to seventy, we ought to consider ourselves lucky to be among the living. There were many times we could have shifted to be among the dead, plenty of risky things we undertook, plenty of illnesses to which we could have succumbed but here we are, still among the living. The sketch on well-being provides some insights into how we might continue to reside among the living although at some moment in the future we will stop and we will be dead.

We have had a long time to contemplate death. Some of us are afraid of it, while others of us remain circumspect. For most of us, it is the imagination of loss that makes us sad. We can imagine we won't see our children or our children's children grow into adults; we won't do the things we still have planned; we won't have our affairs in order; and we'll no longer be able to be part of the life that we lived for so long. If we're religious, we'll believe there's another life, there's a resurrection and a life everlasting. We may believe we'll all be together again someday but in a different form. Our death is something we ought to be able to live with and prepare for without getting all maudlin or depressed.

French writer Philippe Ariès wrote extensively about death and Western attitudes towards it. It's a very interesting work, one which places in context how we have from early times changed our attitudes towards our death. Ariès' research culminated in a book entitled *The Hour of Our*

Death: the classic history of western attitudes toward death over the last thousand years. Ariès spent more than twenty years thinking about changes in Western attitudes from early Christian times, arguing that in those early times death was too common to be frightening. By the eleventh century, when a sense of self began to surface, death meant the destruction of self rather than simply a weakening of community. Here came the first attempts, through rituals, to offer a life in the next world. Today, if we believe in nothing more than that when we die we cease to exist, we are following early Greco-Roman thought. Ariès is also keen to show that during the twentieth century we banished death from our daily lives. It has now become something abstract, something that happens to other people and if it does happen to those close to us, it's to be taken as lightly as it was a thousand years ago – pay your respects and move on.

How do we feel about death by the time we reach the age of seventy? Have we ever given it much thought? Do we consciously do things so that we might avoid death? Can we avoid death? We cannot in fact avoid death. It comes to all of us. How we go about stretching our lives for the longest possible time is what we do. Not too many people want to die. Nine people will kill themselves today as you read this book. Seven of them will be men. Most of us, however, have an innate sense of wanting to remain with the living.

Some of us smoke and some of us drink too much and our medical person tells us that these things are not good for us and will in fact kill us but we keep right on doing them. It may be a gambler's fatal attraction to the unknown which keeps smokers and drinkers going. We eat too many fatty foods and we don't exercise enough, all the things mentioned in other sketches that contribute to an early demise.

I remember my father some years ago being overjoyed because he had reached the age of seventy-six, which was then the average for an Australian male. He must have thought that was enough because he lived only five years more. He was seventy-six in 1997. Since then, almost a generation has passed and the average life expectancy for men is now eighty-three.

If eighty-three is an average age, then we seventy-year-olds can expect to live until we're what, 110? Not quite. The average age is for males born now rather than in the early 1950s. For us, the life expectancy at birth is seventy. Yoiks! That's a world average which takes into account all those countries with low life expectancy. Australian men born in the early 1950s could expect to live to sixty-eight. If you lived to forty-five, it got better; you could expect to live until you were seventy-two.

If you made it over sixty-five, then you could expect to live to seventy-eight. So if you've already made it to seventy, you'll probably do as Clive Palmer and Robin Williamson suggest and be living a great long time: eighty-three or more. How good is that? If you'd been born in the Greco-Roman era, you might not have made it passed thirty. If you made it to ten in late mediaeval England, you could expect to live for another twenty years, and if you got to twenty-five, then you had another twenty-three to go. In the eighteenth century, forty was a long life. But what do you need to think about when you get to the hour of your death?

We're interested in how we as seventy-year-olds approach death and prepare for death. Does it mean writing a will, buying a pre-paid funeral, buying a plot, either a hole in a wall or a grave? Those practical things probably ought to be done by you rather than leaving them to others. When my father-in-law died at the age of ninety-six, he had put in place those practical things but it still took months for his offspring to get their acts together and sort out probate. It took many more months for them to sort out his finances and sell his house. They were not so much incompetent as not prepared for what needed to be done. And they went off on holidays so that the requirement of all three of them to sign things took longer and longer. And all the time the inheritance was providing others with bank interest and costing them money to maintain the house. Not a good look.

It could have been managed much better if the old man had taken control of his affairs, financial and property, and consolidated them rather than having bank passbook accounts and other archaic things floating around. But these are the tangible things we can do to ease our minds before the precipice is at hand. It's when we're on the precipice that we must confront the reality that is death. Aside from the possibility of being killed in some type of accident, of killing ourselves or of having a fatal heart attack, the question we might think about is what are the signs of death and will we know when we are about to die?

Some years ago, I knew a woman whose friend was dying from cancer. Her comment was that the medical profession had made its diagnosis and there was no hope of her continuing to live, yet she still held out hope. Hope is what we apply to the continued need to live but it doesn't help us much with the actuality of death. We know a lot of men who are no longer living. We still know them even though they're dead; they don't cease to be part of our lives. But we knew them from our observations of them, not because we were them. We have only our experience of watching them die, not their experience of dying, to help us with our own death. They may have imparted to us how they felt, what thoughts they had, what emotions they experienced at certain times as they navigated their course. But in the end, they died their own deaths and all we could do was watch.

I recall a neighbour who maintained an air of bravado as he navigated the early symptoms of stomach cancer. As the end drew near, his body became wretched and his mind wandered as more and more morphine was pumped in to him. For some reason, he wanted to die at his home, which I felt placed an unwanted burden on his wife. For her part, she nursed him, then the day after he died she ordered a skip bin and dumped all his books, his porn videos and his clothes and furniture in it, found herself a new man and promptly sold his house and moved. So what was the benefit of dying at home? Did he think it would cement her to the place?

Another man I knew years later and for about the same time, suffered the same disease. They were both in their early sixties when they died. The second one showed no bravado, no talk of fighting it. He didn't live long after he was diagnosed. He did say he should not have gone overseas on holiday, ignoring the stomach pains. But by then it was too late. Neither of these men claimed to have faith. Neither attended church nor believed in God. They died without the benefit of religious succour. I spent a bit of time with them talking about things. Nothing important. Nothing significant. It was as if they had made peace with themselves and the inevitable nature of their deaths.

Before my father died, he had lived with me for six months. He was suffering from liver cancer and was unable to continue looking after himself. He should have come to me earlier but he was stubborn and humble; he did not want to impose himself on me and my wife and children for what then may have seemed like an open-ended timeframe. I would sit with him after dinner when he was taking his medication. His mind was very foggy by the later stages of the disease and he would become anxious about the fact that he thought he hadn't taken the medication even though I said I'd just seen him do it. It wasn't as if he didn't trust me; it was that he didn't trust himself.

Towards the end, when he spent two days in a hospice, I sat with him and held his hand. Then I said something I still can't reconcile. I said, 'Wherever you go from here, wait for me.' In what he had left of his voice, he said okay, and without opening his eyes he continued to hold my hand. I left on the last day to go home and have dinner. I was called back a few hours later as the physician said my father had not much longer to live. I still don't know how he knew, even though he explained to me that by pinching his earlobe and receiving no response the body was shutting down.

I sat with my father until one thirty the next morning when he stopped breathing. That was it. There was nothing else. He simply stopped breathing. Life was extinguished and he was in death. I sat with him a little longer until I felt an exhaustion come over me so that I had to leave and drive home. For a long time afterwards, many months in fact, I felt that I wanted to go with him. It was as if a part of me that I had had all my life had been taken away and it was never coming back.

I didn't feel quite the same when my mother died thirteen years earlier. I had always been close to her but what I felt on the death of my father I have never felt with any other man or woman who has died. I think about him a lot. About the poor relationship we had when I was a teenager. About how he was unable, as the product of his own father's suicide when he was eleven, to provide a lot of fatherliness because he had no basis from which to draw it. About how he was always there for me, even if I wasn't conscious of it: the times when the car broke down, as I described earlier, and later when his grandchildren arrived, how much joy he took from them. I was in the middle between son and father for sixteen years and I would describe them as some of the best years of my own life. I could feel the dynamic of seeing my father growing older and my son growing up. I'm now on the far end, as he was, and I begin to understand how he felt about a great number of things not least of which was his own death.

If we can look at death, at the end of a good life, without fear or dread, then we're probably ready to accept it. We may not wish it to arrive but at the very least we will be ready when it does. The Church of England's Book of Common Prayer has some significance when it comes to death, as do other religious tracts.

As an Anglican, the BCP holds more immediacy for me. So I include here two passages. The first, 'I am the resurrection and the life, sayeth the Lord: he that believeth in me, though he were dead, yet shall he live: and whosoever liveth and believeth in me shall never die.' The second I discovered on the headstone of my great-great-grandparents' grave not all that many years ago. For various reasons, my family lost their historical connections. The inscription reads, 'I know that my Redeemer liveth and he shall stand at the latter day upon the earth.'

For me, as I age, there is more resonance in these words than there may have been when I was younger. I don't advocate for any particular religion nor do I suggest anyone ought to consider adopting a religious posture. For me, however, there is a degree of comfort in the Anglican Book of Common Prayer and the King James Bible which help me to face the prospect of the hour of my own death.

Conclusions & Intentions

A manifesto, by its nature, must telegraph its intentions. Conclusions, on the other hand, are what we draw from what has been written. A conclusion might be that seventy is not what it's cracked up to be. It might also be that things are not as bad as they seem and the future has some prospects of 'being'. If not glorious, then satisfactory.

I believe that being seventy is not the end of the road. It is not a time for standing on the precipice looking into the abyss. Nor is it time to lie down and wait for the end to arrive. It is, though, a time for reflection, not on the past, but on the future. It is a matter of applying your reflections to how you want to live out the remainder of your life. In this, there are many and varied layers for you to consider. Ability and disability play huge roles from here on.

Want to go and climb a few Munros? Then get on a plane to Scotland, head in to Cotswold Outdoors, buy yourself a warm jacket, a pair of boots, a medium-sized rucksack and get to it. Got an inkling to fly-fish in Montana? Walk around the base of Chamonix? Drive out in to the Tanami Desert? Buy a motorbike and tour around New Zealand? Shoot a bear? Well, you probably won't want to shoot a bear, although some years back I knew younger men in North Carolina who went on a few bear hunts. Shooting bears is not really on your list. You actually don't have a list because at seventy you've done pretty much everything you want to do except shoot a bear. We'll leave the bear alone.

What I'm interested in here is what you can do within your physical and financial capabilities. I have a mate who has a mate who goes off around the world fishing. Spends an inordinate sum to chase different species, yet he won't go offshore on the far south coast of NSW when his mate has a boat and an open invitation. Likes fishing. Gets seasick.

You can make a list if you like but make it one you can manage, otherwise you're going to give yourself hypertension because you can't actually do anything on the list. Forget fly-fishing in Montana. Scratch walking around Chamonix or any other popular walking route in Europe as they're stuffed chock-full of moronic Millennials taking selfies and being absorbed by their own existences.

A motorbike could be a genuine go. Doesn't have to be a new one. Although if you can afford it, new will keep you on the road better. What you don't need as a seventy-year-old is to spend time fixing your machine in some Back o' Bourke joint where the only beer is warm West End that costs $10 a tin. Plan your ride.

What about the 4x4 into the desert? Not a bad idea. Take your dog if you have one. If you don't, think about getting one. Good company. Stands guard at night. But if you're thinking about going from motel to motel, pooch could be a problem. Then when you get back could be another problem. Do you want a dog hanging around? Costly mongrels.

The Munros might be the best idea. Hop on a bomber, land in London, have lunch at the Savoy Grill, then, depending upon your desire, train it to Edinburgh or fly. Stay a few nights at the Balmoral then hire a car. Go to Blackwell's and buy a guide book to the Munros, head off towards Inverness and begin. At Blackwell's, you might also buy a copy of Isaak Walton's *The Compleat Angler* for a bit of after-dinner reading. It may give you some thoughts about fishing for salmon while you're there. It's been in print as long as the Holy Bible, so it must be a reasonably good read. If the moronic Millennial in the bookshop says they don't have it, spell Compleat for her. Then spend a nice few days on the Spey with a bottle of Speyside single malt. It could turn into a bit of an epic.

Better get an open-ended return ticket. And don't skimp. At seventy, there won't be too many more long-haul flights left in you. Make it business class, but if you can't extend to that, at least give extended economy a shot. It's not much better than economy. Second thoughts, business. Forget the expense. There's only one of you and you deserve it. Wait. We haven't mentioned the possibility of a 'trailing spouse'. This is the person you take with you when you go somewhere. Let's fantasise for a moment that you're going it alone.

So far we've signalled our intentions in terms of physical well-being and the ability to travel long distances. That would be a pleasant state of affairs and one we might very well be able to pull off. You might have noticed by now the focus of the manifesto is still wallowing around in dreams and desires rather than real-world possibilities.

In the real world of the seventy-year-old, all the things you told yourself you were going to leave behind – all the concerns, all the problems, all the dysfunctional relationships, all the ailments and all the good stuff – are still there. You told yourself you were being rid of them but you forgot to tell everyone in your life. You don't live in isolation. Well, some men do, sadly, and their isolation is an indictment of the poor state of our national consciousness.

Today the world is focused on women. If you live in the Middle east, Africa or South America, pretty much anywhere other than the Western world, being a man is not something to be ashamed of. And being an old man is, in fact, respected.

We spend a lot of time these days talking about Aboriginal elders and how important they are to Indigenous society but of equal importance are white elders, men who for generations have been looked up to and whose advice and council were seen as being of value. The problem we have is that we're no longer valued. Some very powerful elements in our society have invested much time and effort to portray us as the 'problem', so much so that we now find ourselves having to defend our existence as men in the face of accusations that actions that occurred throughout the course of history were our responsibility precisely because we're men. Western society has shifted its perception, so that older white men can no longer speak as men. We must apologise for being who we are. We must defend ourselves against many spurious claims or we'll find ourselves being proscribed to a standstill.

For us as seventy-year-old men, this is a conundrum. We've given away any hope of resurfacing as men. If we act in a manly fashion, we're derided as being dangerous, presenting a poor image for boys, and being misogynists. If we go along with it all and acquiesce, then we're weak and not real men.

Now we're seventy, we're no longer a threat, no longer dangerous (to anyone other than ourselves) and we're not responsible for the ills visited on the world throughout history. Two of the ways we can correct this is to present a dignified and mature image of ourselves to the world. We have opinions and ideas. We have seventy years' worth of knowledge and mental acuity. We must demonstrate to the world that we, seventy-year-old men, whether we are white, black or any shade in between, are still here and we're not going anywhere (well, not just yet if we can avoid it). By all means, rage against the dying of the light, but at the same time go out, buy some heavy-duty batteries, stick them in a powerful torch and shine the bugger right back at them. In a dignified, mature and manly fashion. That will be the first step on the dirt road that has a long, long way yet to run.

Let's tie this up with a few observations that may make out intentions as seventy-year-olds more appealing. Even the best intentions can be knocked sideways by the most insignificant thing. We need to keep our focus and push through all the detritus that has built up over the years. Layers of insignificance can build up until we feel there's no way past, no way to get out into open ground.

Sometimes, we get stopped by our own thoughts or combination of thoughts, especially when those thoughts involve others. I worked some years ago in Philadelphia with a person who constantly erected hurdles that made my job difficult. A friendly colleague had a simple solution. Step around them, he said. There are plenty of impacts on our lives that are not of our own doing. And much as we might like to bugger off and leave them to their own devices, we have responsibilities which are impossible to avoid.

One of the things we need to do is to not so much escape our responsibilities permanently but we ought to spend time away from them, alone if possible, or if you're already spending too much time alone, then with a group of like-minded souls. Seventy means you have access to some pretty reasonable travel concessions. Get on a train or a bus and go somewhere for a few days. If you have a car, leave it at home. Book an airbnb or a room in a pub. Walk around town, have a few quiet ales, a good steak, then get back on the train or bus a day or so later. Make it a long run. Sydney to Broken Hill; Melbourne to Mildura; Brisbane to Townsville. Doesn't need to be some fiesta or carnival of grotesques that you're going to. Just go. And don't fall for those pretty advertisements for seniors. Don't plan it; just do it. Spare shirt. Spare pair of underpants. Spare socks. Probably don't even need the socks. And forget about the idea of being robbed of your spontaneity. Have a crack.

Let's conclude by looking at some of the good eggs and some of the odd fish. We know the good eggs. They're our mates and our mates mates. Good blokes, or good old boys as the Americans like to call them. Very much out of favour these days because these good blokes and good old boys have been labelled. Toxic masculinity springs to mind. But how toxic is the mate who drops everything and minds his grandson so his daughter and son-in-law can go out for dinner? How toxic is the bloke who takes his wife to hospital for her annual cardio stress test, waits for her, then drives her home and makes her lunch?

How toxic is the bloke who sells his house and moves in with his son and daughter-in-law and their kids so they can have the financial capacity to live reasonably decent lives? How toxic is the…et cetera, Well, not toxic at all if men go about doing good. Good eggs. Leftie activist feminists can invent labels for them but the good eggs remain just that – good eggs.

What about the odd fish? Odd is not the opposite of good. The definition of an odd fish is a very strange person. This book was originally entitled *Good Eggs & Weird Fish* but a mate used the expression odd fish when referring to one of his own mates. When I asked him if he meant weird fish, he said no, the expression was odd fish. And it makes more sense in a funny sort of way. Leave out the fish bit and odd is far more appropriate for a lot of seventy-year-old men than weird. Weird can mean strange, unusual or unexpected, while odd means strange or unusual. Wait. They have the same meaning. One, however, has stronger connotations than the other. 'He's a bit odd' is not nearly so severe as 'he's a bit weird'.

There are a lot of seventy-year-old odd fish. My mate's mate, for example. If I were to think about it for too long and to think about some of the things my mates do and how they live their lives, I would have to agree that the majority of them are indeed odd fish. Some of them have lived with their wives for a very long time. Others have been divorced, some are widowers and they all, including me, at times, do very odd things. So we can be Good Eggs and Odd Fish at the same time, if you like. In parallel.

We can describe ourselves as both because we have nothing to lose. It's more about what others think of us and how they see us that shapes our lives and gives us anxiety or worries us so that we get hypertense. High blood pressure gives us all sorts of physical ailments, so that we begin to concentrate on the ailments and forget that it was the image of ourselves that we think other people have that got us anxious in the first place.

Instead of shrugging it off and not caring what people think of us, we tend to get bogged down in the worry of how we might look. Well, if you've lived for seventy years, then you deserve to treat yourself to the luxury of not caring about what others think. By that I don't mean who you see looking back at you when you look in the mirror in the morning. I mean the broader world in which you live. Does it matter what the kid at Hammer Barn thinks of you when you return that reciprocating saw because you bought it on a whim? Does it matter what the assistant thinks of you when you go into a menswear shop to try on new clothes? Of course not. What matters is how you feel and whether you feel comfortable with the decisions you make regarding yourself and those around you.

Think about it like this. What would be your first reaction if you saw someone on the street keel over clutching their arm or chest? Capture it on your phone? Of course not. You would get to them as fast as you could and render assistance. The first-responder assistance may be limited to calling an emergency number and sitting with the person giving them comfort or if they are not breathing, or it may be CPR. The Good Egg in you takes over. Your subconscious takes over and the Good Egg surfaces. We are all Good Eggs and Odd Fish and the world needs us.

www.ingramcontent.com/pod-product-compliance
Lightning Source LLC
Chambersburg PA
CBHW071458080526
44587CB00014B/2147